Bags, Boxes, Buttons, and Beyond with The Bag Ladies

A Resource Book of Science and Social Studies Projects for K–6 Teachers, Parents, and Students

written by

The Bag Ladies

Cindy Guinn and Karen Simmons

illustrated by

Cindy Guinn

Maupin House

Bags, Boxes, Buttons, and Beyond with The Bag Ladies:
A Resource Book of Science and Social Studies Projects for K-6 Teachers, Parents, and Students

© 2004 Cindy Guinn and Karen Simmons

Cover and book design and illustrations: Cindy Guinn
Photography: Donna Purtell
Typesetting: Maria Messenger

Library of Congress Cataloging-in-Publication Data

Guinn, Cindy, 1959-
  Bags, boxes, buttons, and beyond with the Bag Ladies : a resource book of science and social studies projects for K-6 teachers, parents, and students / written by The Bag Ladies, Cindy Guinn and Karen Simmons ; illustrated by Cindy Guinn.
       p. cm.
Includes bibliographical references and index.
  ISBN 0-929895-72-X (pbk.)
1. Science--Study and teaching (Elementary)--Activity programs--United States. 2. Social sciences--Study and teaching (Elementary)--Activity programs--United States. 3. Interdisciplinary approach in education--United States. I. Simmons, Karen, 1948- II. Title.
  LB1585.3.G85 2004
  372.3'5--dc22

                                                                 2003022083

ISBN-10: 0-929895-72-X
ISBN-13: 978-0-929895-72-7

10 9 8 7 6 5 4

Also by The Bag Ladies:

A Bookbag of The Bag Ladies' Best
Math, Manipulatives, and Magic Wands

Contact The Bag Ladies directly for workshop and conference appearances at bladies123@aol.com.

Special Thanks to: Donna Purtell, whose photography makes us look good and whose creativity makes our projects stand out. Tim Mason, who tries to keep us organized. Our model photographer, Leuwann Price, and our models: Peyton Ellis, Caleb Weier, Samantha Stein, Sophie Price, and Helen Price. Our entire Beacon Cove Intermediate Family and all our "bagettes," our students who make learning come alive with bags, boxes, buttons, and so much more.

Maupin House publishes professional resources that improve student performance. Inquire about scheduling on-site training, author visits, or about ordering resources.

Maupin House
PO Box 90148
Gainesville, FL 32607
Phone: 800-524-0634 or 352-373-5588
Fax: 352-373-5546
E-mail: info@maupinhouse.com

www.maupinhouse.com

Dedication

To Greg for his love, help, and understanding. CG

To Aunt Jean, my godmother who always said, "Believe in yourself!" CG

To Gene, Josh, and Jesse, who inspire me every day with their love and pride in what I do. KS

To our Beacon Cove "Family" for their encouragement and support. KS/CG

Welcome

Dear Educator,

With great pride, we present our third book: *Bags, Boxes, Buttons, and Beyond.* We are teachers first; our love of teaching prompted us to start writing thematic units with hands-on activities, enhanced with literature to motivate students. These units—each stored in a bag—allowed us to present "make-n-take" workshops throughout Florida and across the United States in order to raise teachers' enthusiasm about teaching. Our first book, *A Bookbag of the Bag Ladies' Best,* was a collection of The Bag Ladies' ideas and hands-on projects that helped students of all abilities learn skills across the curriculum in a fun way. Our second book, *Math, Manipulatives, and Magic Wands,* incorporated these same types of projects but added manipulatives based on teaching the standards of the National Council of Teachers of Mathematics.

In this third book, we introduce models that will allow you and your students to organize whatever theme you're working on into a functional activity package that grows as students move through a unit. These include the bag "holders" and projects, box projects, button projects, and many more hands-on activities, all using various easy-to-find materials. We have suggested ways to use these projects in science and social studies, but you can easily incorporate these applications into any standard of the curriculum. We write our books for students from K–6 and believe that the same projects can be used for all levels. You will just see a different "look" to the projects.

Being teachers has helped us to write this book with YOU in mind. We include stories and solutions to daily questions you have about classroom management, time, assessments, and budgets. And we know that you'll identify with the teaching styles of The Bag Ladies as you watch student achievement and motivation rise.

Lastly, we hope that these projects help you and your students continue learning in a fun, exciting way.

Love,
The Bag Ladies

Table of Contents

Project Page Format

Materials needed:

All the materials you need will be listed here. Materials are listed per student, not per class. You will need to multiply the number listed by the number of students in your class. Suggestions on where to purchase the materials are also provided at the beginning of each section.

Instructions:

Step-by-step directions on how to complete each make-n-take activity will be listed here.

Blackline masters have been provided for some of the activities.

Social Studies and Science:

For many of our projects, we provide three suggested activities for both social studies and science. Remember these are only suggestions, you will think of many more great ways to use these projects throughout the school year.

Diagrams:

We have included drawings of each step to help you create the activity. Like they say, "a picture's worth a thousand words." When needed, we have also included photographs of some of the projects so you can see what a finished project looks like.

Project Rubric

Effort-How much time was put into the project? Is it quality work for this student?

Creativity-Students are encouraged to use their own ideas to add to the project.

Mastery of the Standard-Does the student demonstrate that he/she understands the skill?

Followed Directions-Did the student follow written and verbal directions?

Neatness-How neat is the finished product?

Completeness-Is all information included?

Assessment Scale		Total Points	
A= 90-100	4 points	outstanding work	21 to 24 points
B= 80-89	3 points	good work	16 to 20 points
C= 70-79	2 points	fair work	11 to 15 points
D= 60-69	1 point	you can do better	6 to 10 points
F= below 60	0 points	upgradeable	0 to 5 points

_____

Name_____Date_____

Points Earned

_____ Effort
_____ Creativity
_____ Mastery of Standards
_____ Followed Directions
_____ Neatness
_____ Completeness

_____ TOTAL = GRADE_____

Literature

Literature plays a big role in how we teach every subject. Whether we are beginning a unit in science or social studies, or teaching a skill lesson in those subjects, we start with a great book. When reading the book, our enthusiasm motivates students to get excited about the next theme or lesson. Reading literature also prompts students to ask questions, seek out more of the same types of books, and get curious about what they will learn.

We usually gather all of the students in one area of the room where everyone can sit and enjoy the reading of our "favorite" book. They look forward to this routine. We find that the intermediate students love "picture books" as much as the primary students do. Many of these books are geared for the more mature students. We are sure that you will find your own "favorites" to add to the lists! Keep them in a bin near your models and folders, and everything will be ready for use from year to year.

Here is a list of some of our favorite books and authors. These literature lists pertain to all classes K through 6. Use these at the beginning of the unit, during the unit as you introduce concepts and projects, and at the end of the unit when you review and wrap up.

* Note that some of these content-area books overlap and could be used for either science or social studies, depending on the lesson topic.

Literature for Science

A Tree is Nice, Janice Udry
Buster's Adventure Series, John Harms II
50 Simple Things Kids Can Do to Save the Earth, The Earthworks Group
Flicker Flash, Joan Bransfield Graham
How to Eat Fried Worms, Thomas Rockwell
In the Tall, Tall Grass, Denise Fleming
Just a Dream, Chris Van Allsburg
Miss Rumphius, Barbara Cooney
Moe the Dog in Tropical Paradise, Diane Stanley and Elise Primavera
Mohave, Diane Siebert
Mole's Hill: A Woodland Tale, Lois Ehlert
Nuts to You!, Lois Ehlert
Over the Steamy Swamp, Paul Geraghty
Planting a Rainbow, Lois Ehlert
Rain, Robert Kalan
Round the Garden, Omri Glaser
Q is for Quark: A Science Alphabet Book, David M. Schwartz
Sam the Sea Cow, Francine Jacobs

Sylvester and the Magic Pebble, William Steiger
The Burrowing Book, DK Publishing
The Desert is Theirs, Byrd Baylor
The Magic School Bus, Science Chapter Book Series, Eva Moore
The Rain Came Down, David Shannon
The Salamander Room, Anne Mazer
The Talking Earth, Jean Craighead George
Thunder Cake, Patricia Polacco
Tops and Bottoms, Janet Stevens
Tracks in the Sand, Loreen Leedy
Tree of Life: The World of the African Baobab, Barbara Bash
Very Quiet Cricket, Eric Carle
Wolves, Gail Gibbons
Wonderful Worms, Linda Glaser

Literature for Social Studies

A is for America, Devon Scillian
Antler Bear Canoe: A North Woods Alphabet Year, Betsy Bowen
Are We There Yet, Daddy? Virginia Walters
Eight Hands Round: A Patchwork Alphabet, Patricia Polacco
Gleam and Glow, Eve Bunting
Habitat: Life Underground, Maria Ruif
Hieroglyphics from A to Z, Peter De Manuelian
Mummies Made in Egypt, Aliki
Oonawassee Summer, Melissa Forney
Renchenka's Eggs, Patricia Polacco
S is for Sunshine: A Florida Alphabet Book, Carol Crane
Samantha's Ocean Liner Adventure, Dottie Raymer
Santaclaustrophobia, Mike Reiff
State Book Series, Sleeping Bear Press
Thank You, Mr. Falker, Patricia Polacco
The Alaska Alphabet Book, Charlene Kreeger and Shannon Cartwright
The Gift, Marcia S. Freeman
The History Puzzle, Cherry Denman
The Magic Tree House Series, Mary Pope Osborne
The Memory String, Eve Bunting
The Name Jar, Yangsook Choi
The Quiltmaker's Gift, Jeff Brumbeau
The Skull Alphabet Book, (and others) by Jerry Pallotta
The Teacher's Book of Lists, Sheila Madsen and Bette Gould

Bags

This summer I visited the grocery store.
I begged for bags;
They gave me four.

"But, I'm using them for children's sake—
Holders and projects, we will make."
"Oh, you're a teacher," the clerk replied,
As he tiptoed into his office to hide.

Well, bags are sturdy, just like me.
I'll think of a way to get more than three,
And I'll think of a way to get them for free!

They will show students how to organize—
20, 12, or 8 pouches of all size.
We'll shape and glue and cut and pleat
Then using the standards, we'll repeat.

But learning and teaching will now be fun.
So find those bags;
Learning has begun!

—The Bag Ladies

The Bag Holders

Which came first: The Bag Ladies or the bags?

Many people think that we are called The Bag Ladies because we make everything from bags. This is incorrect. We make our standard-based activities from many easy-to-find materials. We actually chose the name because of the fact that we housed our many thematic units in bags. What's more, if you ever watch teachers arrive at school in the morning, they are loaded down with tote bags. (What do we carry in all of those things anyway?!) So, the name "The Bag Ladies" became our trademark. However, upon consideration, we decided that maybe using bags wasn't such a bad idea. They are durable, easy to obtain, and cheap. Best of all, bags can be folded and cut into many practical holders for student work. Now we are truly "The Bag Ladies."

Why bag holders?

Through years of making hands-on projects with our students, we found that they needed a way to keep these activities and study projects together in one grouping. How many times have you checked students' desks looking for a missing paper, only to find the insides of the desks "wallpapered" with those same papers? For this reason, we have created "bag holders," made and shaped to hold projects, activities, and writing responses as students move through a unit of study. From fanny packs with tabbed dividers to flat-top backpacks or travel bags, students are motivated to create organizational pouches that hold it all. But just like Rome, these aren't built in a day, so let's start with…

Getting the materials together

If you are like The Bag Ladies you can't go to your local grocery store and beg for bags anymore. The kind manager has given you the last bag, and when he sees you come through the door he hides in his office until you leave. Plan B is to buy the bags in bulk from discount stores or warehouses. You'll find they are very reasonably priced and come in all sizes. And as we all know, cost is important because teachers across the country receive the same buck-ninety-eight allowance for their yearly budget, so we have to be creative!

Other materials you'll need for the holders:

* Gel FX® markers—these markers, designed for construction paper, write on all colors and make the brown-bag art work "pop out." You can buy them at discount and craft stores.

* A packaging-tape dispenser and good quality, clear, wide packaging tape. Just forget what we said about cost effectiveness here. Only the stronger tape will last. In this case, you really do get what you pay for.
* Pipe cleaners in all colors, chicken rings (ask about them at your local feed shop), and survey tape (the neon-colored tape also known as crime-scene tape) found at Home Depot.
* Super grip hole punchers—OK, one more splurge, but these are incredible! They will last all year and make those hard-to-reach places accessible. We bought ours at an office supply store, and they have dark blue, cushioned handles.
* Velcro—the kind with a sticky back side.

Before students begin making their holders, it's your turn.

Getting started

We begin each new theme with great literature and an introduction that motivates students about their next area of study. Then we show a "model" of the holder they will make. Complete your own decorated model to show students what a finished product looks like. Making your own model will also help you understand the easiest way to present it to your class.

Purchase and stack all materials listed on the page so that they're ready to be passed out to your students. Remember, this is not a one day activity. Divide the project into smaller parts to prevent students and you from becoming frustrated. Keep it risk-free by following the next steps.

Tips for making the bag holders

When guiding students step-by-step, we give one step in the directions, then say, "Now you," which prompts students to listen first, then begin. This helps in all areas of following directions. Move slowly through the steps and walk around the classroom with the model. Try to recruit two volunteers (parents or older students) to help on the day you make the holders. Students will also help each other.

Set up a table in the back of the room if there is a step that must be done with an adult or partner. This way a few students can come back and work with a partner, then help others.

Store the special Gel FX® or comparable markers in groups of eight inside small, clear, plastic bags, placing two packs near each group of desks. Collect and recount the markers at the end of the period.

Keep all of your supplies in stacked, plastic containers that are labeled for easy access while making projects.

If all else fails, when a student makes a mistake, give him/her a new bag. After all, it's just a bag.

Classroom Management

People sometimes think that making projects is a noisy, unstructured time in the classroom. The teacher must ensure that students obey the same classroom rules that they use throughout the day with minor adjustments. We tell our classes that they can help each other quietly while making the holders, but we ask that they work silently while decorating them. If you set limits to noise and consistently demand that students follow the rules, the calmer environment will encourage students to enjoy themselves. Sometimes we also play music while they are working.

Assessment

There are many ways to assess students' work on the holders. We allow students to take their holders home after our part is completed in the classroom to "jazz them up." We then set up a rubric based on our objective for the holder. For example: following directions, creativity, neatness, etc. This way, students learn that their time and effort will be rewarded. We do not give grades for the art work; instead we demonstrate how to make it stand out by drawing in pencil first, then outlining with fine-tip black markers, and coloring with crayons, colored pencils, or gel markers.

Storage

We collect the holders at the end of each class period, and then store them in the stacked containers.

Fanny Pack

Materials needed:

* Brown paper lunch bag
* Clear, wide packaging tape
* Survey tape
* Four 5 in. X 7 in. index cards
* Sticky-note tab labels
* Scissors
* Crayons, markers, or colored pencils

Instructions:

1. Open the bag by putting both hands inside and pressing the pleats outward until flat.

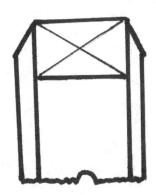

2. Pull the bottom flap to the back and tape down with the clear, wide packaging tape.

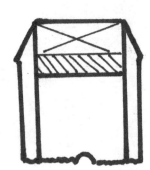

3. Fold the top of the bag toward you, about half way down its length. Cut up both sides of the turned-down flap. Cut off the flap that's underneath, allowing only the top flap to remain.

4. Cut two slits in the back of the bag as illustrated. Insert survey tape into one side and out the other to make a waist strap.

5. Decorate the fanny pack to match a unit of study. For example, research about states or science field experiments.

6. Label and attach a tab to each index card. Place inside fanny pack and use as dividers for vocabulary and note-taking.

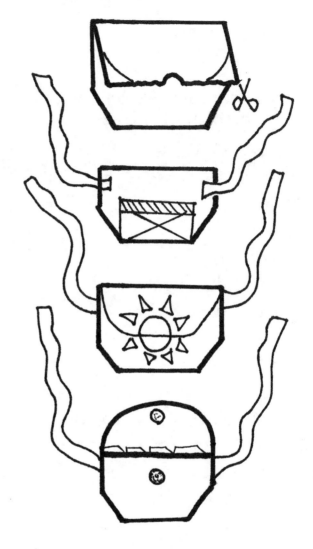

Flat-Top Backpack

Materials needed:

* Two brown paper grocery bags
* One 1/2-inch square of
  sticky-back Velcro®
* Wide, clear packaging tape
* Glue
* Scissors
* Crayons, markers,
  or colored pencils
* 5 feet of survey tape

Instructions:

1. Cut 4 inches off the top of
each bag. Using the clear, wide
packaging tape, tape the
bottom flap of each bag up to
form pockets.

2. Tape the bottom of the
top bag to the top of the
bottom bag.

3. Decorate the pocket on
both the top and the bottom
bags to represent different
unit topics, for example,
Weather and *Environment*.

4. Fold the bags forward, then apply the sticky-back Velcro® to keep them closed together. Cut slits as shown. Thread the survey tape through the slits to create the backpack straps.

5. Decorate the front of the backpack using the crayons, markers, or colored pencils.

6. Throughout the unit, store successive projects in the backpack pockets.

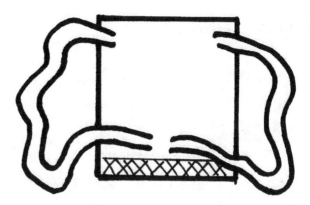

Folder Holder

Materials needed:

* Three brown paper grocery bags
* Three sheets of construction paper (any color) 9 in. X 12 in.
* Clear, wide packaging tape
* Blackline masters of pocket labels (pp. 148–152)
* Crayons, markers, or colored pencils
* Scissors
* Ruler
* Glue

Instructions:

1. Place one brown bag with the flap at the bottom in front of you. Fold the flap down toward the bottom of the bag. Using a ruler, draw a line that's the width of the ruler down the left side of the bag about 12 inches long and repeat down the right side. Then connect the two lines across the bottom.

2. Cut along these lines, cutting through only the top layer of the bag.

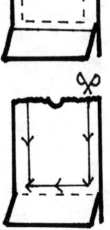

3. Open the bag so it sits up. Cut from the front of the bag around to the side but not through the back. Repeat on the other side of the bag.

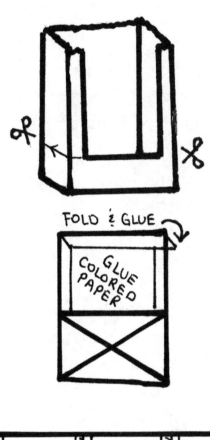

FOLD & GLUE

GLUE COLORED PAPER

4. Collapse the bag and glue a piece of construction paper inside it horizontally, just under the bottom flap. Cut the small flaps off the top, fold down, and glue the top over the construction paper to make a finished edge.

5. Repeat Steps One to Four with the other two bags. Tape the bags together with the wide, clear packaging tape and along the edges to close pockets. Use the pockets to store notes and projects from the unit of study.

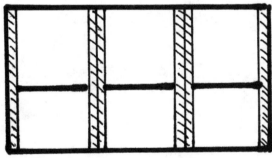

Note Keeper

Materials needed:

* Four brown paper bags of any size
* Clear, wide packaging tape
* Scissors
* Crayons, markers, or colored pencils

Instructions:

1. Cut the bottom flap off of all four brown paper bags.

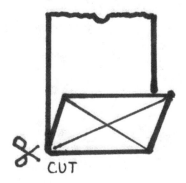

2. Open up the top of each bag and unfold all the side pleats. Stick the clear, wide packaging tape to the bottom of each bag to create the pockets.

3. Lay two bags on top of one another and tape along the left edge by placing half the length of the tape on the top side and folding the remaining tape to the back.

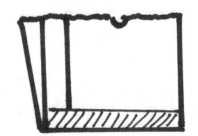

4. Place the next bag on top of the taped bags and tape together with another piece of clear, wide packaging tape in the same manner as before.

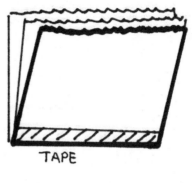

TAPE

5. Repeat this process for the final bag. Using crayons, markers, or colored pencils, label the bags with titles and store important papers and projects in each pocket.

MY NOTE KEEPER

Collecting data

Portfolio One

Materials needed:

* Brown paper grocery bag
* Clear, wide packaging tape
* Crayons, markers, or colored pencils
* Scissors

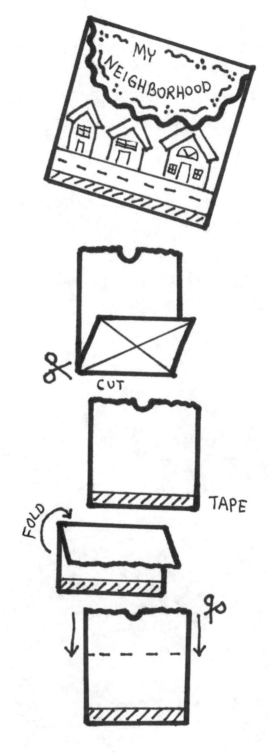

Instructions:

1. Cut the bottom flap off of the bag.

2. Tape the bottom of the bag closed using clear, wide packaging tape.

3. Fold the top of the bag about halfway to the bottom.

4. Open the folded bag and cut a slit down each side to the fold.

5. Fold the flap in the back away from you and cut off the front flap with the tabs attached to it. Refold the remaining flap forward to make a closure for the portfolio.

6. Cut the closure flap by rounding its edges or cutting them with fancy scissors.

7. Open the flap and cut the front layer at a diagonal and across the front. The folded sides of the bag make a natural divider inside the portfolio.

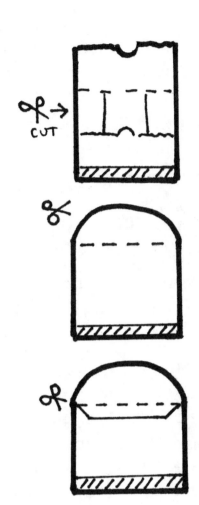

Portfolio Two

Materials needed:

* Brown paper grocery bag
* Scissors
* Three chicken rings
* Hole puncher
* Clear, wide packaging tape
* 1 yard of string
* Two brass paper fasteners
* One large craft foam shape

Instructions:

1. Lay the brown paper grocery bag so the bottom flap is on top. Cut away the bottom edge of flap as shown in the diagram.

2. Place scissors inside the bag and cut up the sides of the bottom flap.

3. Open the bottom flap and pull the triangles forward to make a flat surface.

4. Cut along the vertical edge of the bag and open flat.

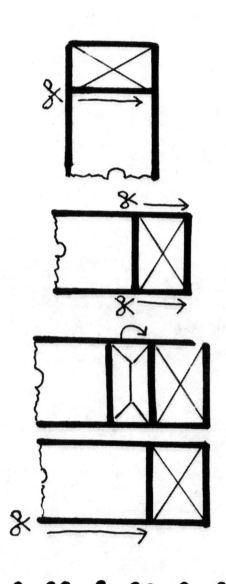

 appears to the right of the instructions.

5. Leave a pleat along the bottom and cut away the extra piece of the bag.

6. Tape the ends closed to form a pocket along the bottom of the bag.

7. Fold the bag in half to the edge of the flap so the pockets are on the inside.

8. Punch three holes along the folded edge and twist chicken rings through them to form a spine similar to a notebook or journal.

9. Cut the edges of the flap off and attach the brass fastener, craft foam, and string. Twist the string around the bag and the shaped craft foam to close the portfolio.

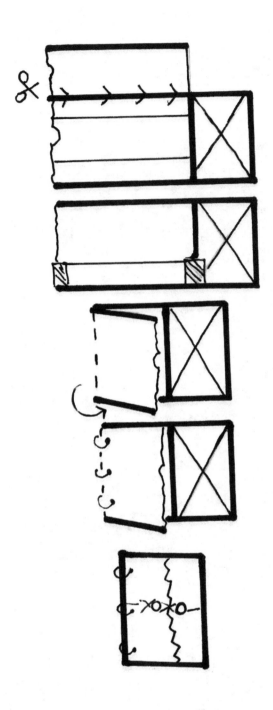

Pouch Project

Materials needed:

* Brown paper grocery bag
* One pipe cleaner
* 1 yard of survey tape
* Two brass fasteners
* 1-inch square of sticky-back Velcro®
* Black marker
* One library pocket
* Scissors
* Hole puncher

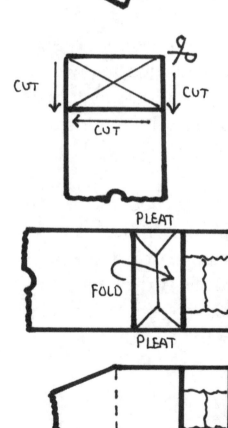

Instructions:

1. Lay the brown paper grocery bag so the bottom flap is showing. Cut the folded edge away on the sides and bottom of the flap as shown.

2. Fold the bottom flap of the bag back. Push the pleats to the center of the bag and push the bottom piece over the pleats.

3. Fold the top of the bag to the top of the flap.

4. Create a decorative bottom flap by rounding its edges. Then fold it down.

5. Open and fold the top of the bag forward. Punch holes through the flap and back side of the pouch. Cut the pipe cleaner in half, then insert this half through the hole. Twist the pipe cleaner into a loop.

6. String survey tape through each pipe-cleaner loop, then tie the ends to create a strap.

7. Attach Velcro® on the inside of the flap to secure the pouch closed.

8. Draw stitches on the pouch using the black marker.

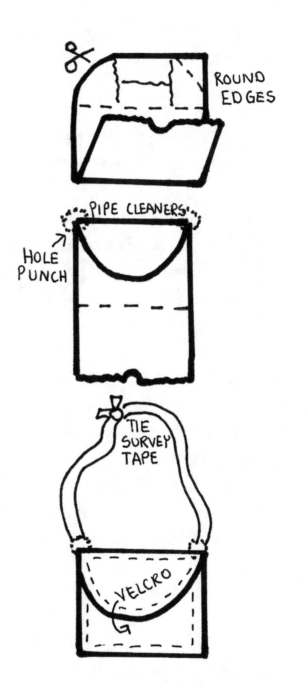

ROUND EDGES

PIPE CLEANERS

HOLE PUNCH

TIE SURVEY TAPE

VELCRO

Travel Bag

Materials needed:

* Scissors
* Brown paper grocery bag
* 2 brass paper fasteners
* 2 craft-foam shapes
* 4-6 inches of thin twine
* Black or brown tempura paint (optional)
* Paint brush
* Hole puncher

Instructions:

1. Lay out the brown paper grocery bag as pictured, with the flap at the bottom. Fold the top of the bag to about 1 inch above the bottom flap.

2. Open to the original position. Cut away all of the top flat of the bag to the fold line except the back layer. Save this piece for later.

3. Round the edges of the remaining flap to form the travel bag's closure flap.

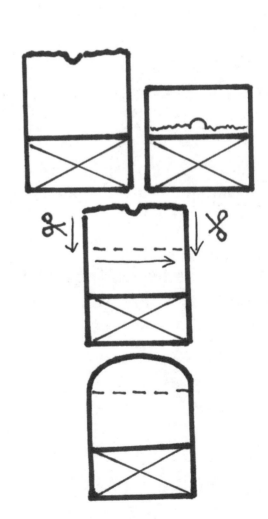

4. Open the scrap that was cut from the front and sides of the bag and fold the two ends to the middle. Fold the bottom up to the middle and the top down over it. This will form a handle for the bag.

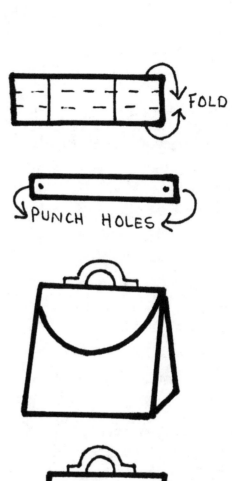

5. Punch a hole at each end of this handle. Push a brass fastener through the holes and attach the handle to the top of the bag on the folded edge. Bring handle in about 1 inch on each side to make stand.

6. To close the bag, attach a craft-foam shape to the flap of the bag with a brass fastener and the other one to the bag itself. Knot the piece of twine around the top craft-foam shape and twist around the bottom shape to close.

7. For a leather-luggage look, crinkle the bag and paint it with watered-down tempera paint.

Tri-Folder

Materials needed:

* Brown paper grocery bag
* Wide, clear packaging tape
* Scissors
* Crayons, markers, or colored pencils

Instructions:

1. Fold the bottom of the bag over its middle as shown in the diagram.

2. Cut the bottom layers away from the top of the bag above the top fold. This will leave one small piece that can be folded forward like a portfolio flap.

3. Cut down the top layer of the bag, stopping at the bottom flap. Then cut across the bag just above the bottom flap in the same manner.

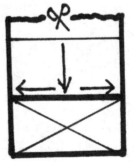

4. Open the remaining part of the bag as if it were a regular paper bag.

5. Cut away the sides of the bag and unfold as shown in the diagram. You will find three equal pieces remaining at the bottom of the bag.

6. Fold the bottom piece up and tape the sides with the clear, wide packaging tape to create a pocket.

7. To close, fold the bottom pocket to the middle and then the middle to the top. Secure with the small flap.

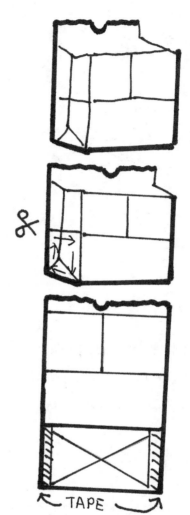

TAPE

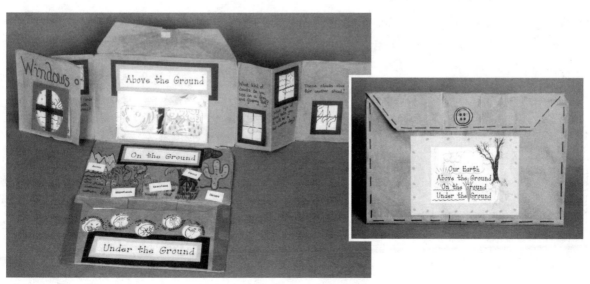

Vest Pocket

Materials needed:

* Brown paper grocery bag
* 1 yard of yarn or string
* Hole puncher
* Scissors
* Crayons, markers, or colored pencils

Instructions:

1. Open the brown paper grocery bag and cut away both side panels, leaving only the front, back, and bottom of the bag attached.

2. Cut across one side of the bag bottom. Fold up the bag bottom and tape it to form a pocket.

3. Place the other piece of the bag on top and cut a "V" to look like the neck of a vest, then round the sides to look like armholes.

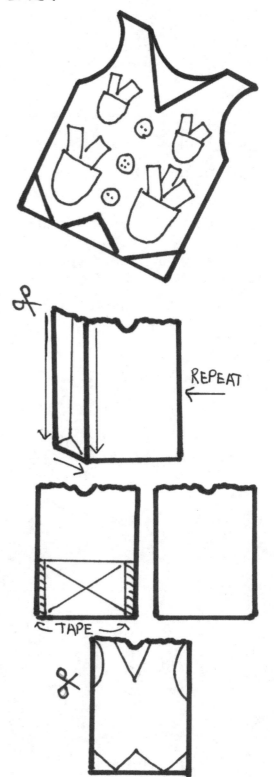

REPEAT

TAPE

4. Punch holes across the top of the bag at the shoulders, then lace the front and back together with the yarn or string.

5. Decorate the front and back of the vest to go with the unit's topic. Students may store projects, notes, and reports inside the pocket.

6. They may want to add more pockets to the front and back of the vest by using library pockets or half of an envelope.

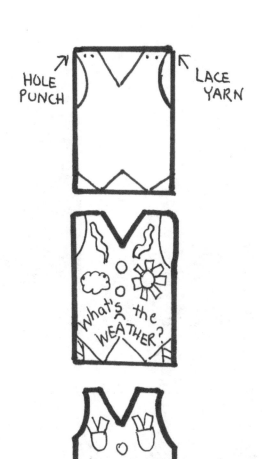

Bag Projects

The Bag Projects

The holder is made, now what?

As you work through the unit of study, you are following your state standards. The projects your students create will be made with one purpose: to help that student apply and retain information for mastery. Here's the sequence we use to teach certain objectives: show a project model, give out materials, and then allow students to get started on their projects. Again, this is a step-by-step process. Students are permitted to work on their projects during free time. This gives you an opportunity to see if students have achieved mastery. The project may be taken home to finish and then turned in for a grade.

Ideas for applications have been given for each bag project in the areas of social studies and science. We have also included blacklines for many of the projects. Most importantly, these projects can be used at any grade level and for any curriculum.

Getting the materials together

Since you bought your bags in bulk, you have plenty left over for your bag projects. Here is a list of items we suggest for your projects:

* Bags of all sizes: 20, 12, 8, grocery size
* Gel FX® Markers (construction paper markers)
* Gift bags, envelopes, Popsicle sticks
* Paper plates—the cheap ones, NOT the grease-resistant ones!
* Brass fasteners, stapler, glue sticks
* Twine, beads, thin wire

How do I get all these materials? Be creative!

We have found many ways to accumulate materials for the projects. We have put 3-dimensional trees in our classrooms, covered them with leaves that name needed supplies, and called it "The Giving Tree." Parents come in and pick a leaf, which holds the name of a classroom material that is needed.

Another way we get donations is by encouraging parents who own their own businesses to "adopt a class." The business gives the teacher $150 to use for classroom supplies.

We have been at schools that permitted grade levels to have their own fundraisers and other schools that ask for donations of materials in their start-of-the-year supply list.

Tips for making the bag projects

The same steps for making projects apply to making the bag holders (see "Tips for making the bag holders," p. 4), BUT student work will now be assessed on a rubric of skills. Did the student demonstrate understanding of a particular objective? Is the project done neatly? Has effort been put into the project? Be sure that students are aware of exactly what they will be graded on for each project as it is presented (see Project Rubric, p. xi). Allow students to be creative in completing the projects.

Presenting the projects to a small group or to the class

It is important for students to present the projects to small groups or to the whole class before taking them home to share and study. Sharing projects allows students to view how others completed the project and gives them time to review the skills that they have worked on throughout the activity.

Storage

After using the activity to prepare for testing and/or assessment, projects are attached to, or kept in, the pockets of the bag holders.

Finally, why do these projects work to reinforce skills?

We believe that these projects work well to motivate students to show their projects, review their projects, and finally study the material presented in each of them. Teachers present these projects in a fun and interesting way that allows students of *all* abilities to creatively learn the objective and how to apply it. Students remember the project, which helps them remember the skill. At the end of the unit, students have a complete "pouch" of skills.

Parents have an opportunity to see what their child is studying, use the activity to help him/her to study, and see creative ways to help their child be excited about studying.

Brown-Bag Accordion Book

Materials needed:

* Brown paper grocery bag
* Scissors
* Crayons, markers, pencils, or colored pencils
* 1 yard of string
* Black fine-tip marker

Instructions:

1. Cut off the bottom flap of the bag. Next, cut down the middle seam and open the bag into a flat strip.

2. Accordion-fold the paper into five equal parts. You may have to trim the end to keep the pages equal in size.

3. Draw the main ideas from the topic selected, using a pencil first. Then trace pencil lines with the black fine-tip marker. Finally, color the illustrations.

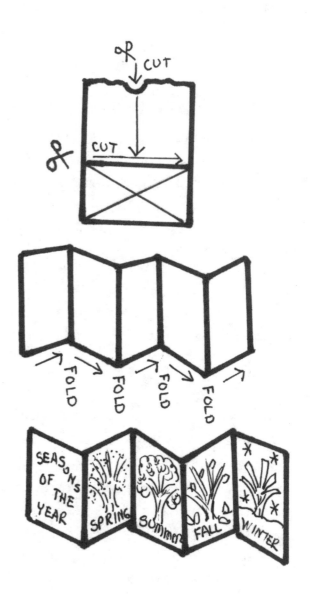

4. You can make multiples of the brown-bag accordion book and tape them together for a longer book.

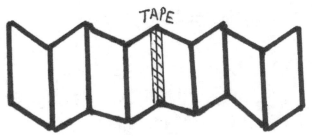

5. You can also punch holes through every other crease and tie a string through them to close the book.

* These books can be made in any size and with any number of pages, depending on the skill being studied and the ability or age of the student. We save scraps from other projects to add pages.

Brown-Bag Journal

Materials needed:

* One 12 in. X 9 in. rectangle of a brown paper grocery bag
* 8 1/2 in. X 11 in. paper
* Black fine-tip marker
* Two 12 in. lengths of thin wire
* Assorted craft beads
* Hole puncher

Instructions:

1. Fold the 12 in. X 9 in. rectangle of brown paper in half horizontally (hamburger fold).

2. Insert the 8 1/2 in. X 11 in. paper inside of the brown paper and punch four holes along the folded edge: the first hole three inches from the top, then down one inch, down two inches, and one more down an inch.

Social Studies:

* Diary of historic events
* Diary of a historic person
* A president's diary

Science:

* Journal an experiment
* Collecting data
* Scientific field guide

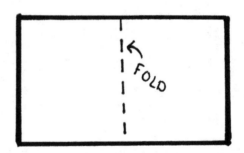

3. Weave the wire through one hole and out the other hole. Twist the wire to secure and add beads to the excess wire. Leave some extra to twist into a spiral so the beads don't fall off the ends. Repeat this process through the second set of holes.

4. The journal is now ready to be personalized with a title, name, and information. On the inside of the journal, dividers can be created to help organize information.

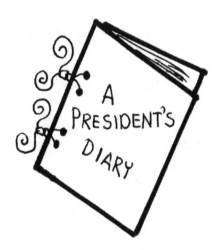

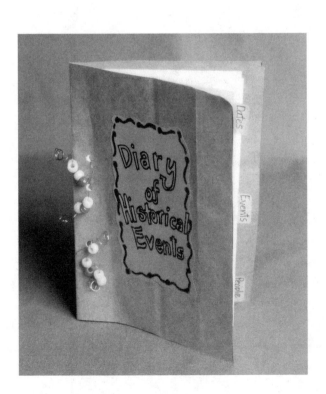

Brown-Bag Stage

Materials needed:

* Brown paper grocery bag
* Crayons, markers, or colored pencils
* Glue
* Scraps of fabric
* Blackline master (p. 153)
* Scissors
* Clear, wide packaging tape

Instructions:

1. Lay out the brown paper bag with the flap side down and on the bottom of bag.

2. Draw a building on this side of the brown paper bag, outline it with black marker, and color. This could be the White House, Empire State Building, or design your own building.

3. Flip the bag over to the flap side and glue the stage blackline to the bag. Color the curtains or glue on material. Cut away the center of the stage through one layer of the bag.

Social Studies:

* Monuments
* Museums
* Building designs

Science:

* Science museum
* Laboratory
* Scientist hall of fame

4. Insert a sheet of paper to serve as the stage background. Decorate the stage background with a landscape scene.

5. Make a slit horizontally across the flap of the bag approximately one inch down from the top of the flap. Tape the sides of the flap up with the packaging tape to form a pocket.

6. Glue a business-size envelope to the flap to store characters. Create characters and attach them to popsicle sticks. To have them perform on the stage, slide them through the slit and up onto the stage.

CHARACTERS

Double-Pocket Autumn Bag

Materials needed:

* Brown paper grocery bag
* Clear, wide packaging tape
* Scissors
* One 11 in. X 17 in. sheet of white paper
* Five 8 1/2 in. X 11 in. sheets of white paper
* Blackline masters (pp.154-156)
* Stapler
* Crayons, markers, or colored pencils
* Assorted colors of tempera paint
* One cotton swab for each color of paint

Instructions:

1. Lay the brown bag flap side up. Using the clear, wide packaging tape, close each edge of the flap to create a pocket.

2. Flip the bag to the plain side without the pocket and cut a pocket in the top, using the tree blackline master as your guide. Only cut through the front layer of the bag.

Social Studies:

* Explorers
* Mayflower
* Transportation

Science:

* Autumn
* Seasons
* Plants

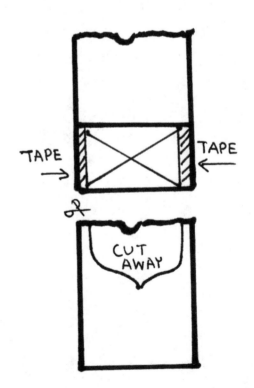

3. Draw and color a tree trunk below the pocket and add a background.

4. Slip the 11 in. X 17 in. paper into the bag, draw branches on the part that is showing. Next, add leaves by dabbing tempera paint on the paper with the cotton swabs.

5. Flip the bag to the opposite side and trace the boat pattern on the pocket of the bag. Decorate it to look like a ship.

6. Use the provided blackline master as a book cover. Staple the blackline master to the sheets of 8 1/2 in. X 11 in. paper to create a book. Draw and write about an ocean voyage and place the book into the pocket.

Gift Bag Book

Materials needed:

* 1 medium size gift bag
  (the type with a handle)
* White paper to fit inside bag
* 3 in. X 3 in. square of
  construction paper
* Scissors
* Stapler
* Glue stick

Instructions:

1. Cut the flap and sides off the bag, leaving the handles in place.

2. Insert the white paper and staple it into the bag along the bottom.

3. Glue the 3 in. X 3 in. piece of construction paper to the front of the book and label.

Social Studies:

* Questions and answers
* Travel journal
* Historic response journal

Science:

* Science vocabulary
* Space travel journal
* Chapter outline journal

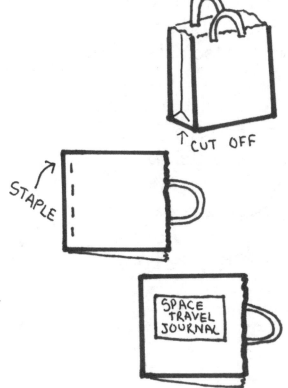

CUT OFF

STAPLE

SPACE TRAVEL JOURNAL

4. Use your gift bag journal to organize social studies or science notes.

5. The journal can be carried by the handles or easily hung on a hook for storage.

* These Gift Bag Books can be made with any size gift bag or shopping bag. Just adjust the size of the paper to be inserted. They also make great book covers for textbooks or hardback books that you want to carry along with you.

Lunch Bag Wallet

Materials needed:

* Brown paper lunch bag
* Scissors
* Cellophane tape
* Crayons, markers, or colored pencils
* 1 in. X 1 in. square of sticky-back Velcro®
* Play money or paper to make currency

Instructions:

1. Fold the bottom of the bag up approximately two inches from the top of the bag.

2. Fold the remaining two inches down and crease. Insert scissors and cut away the bottom layer of the two-inch flap.

3. Cut the corners of the flap at an angle and add Velcro® to close it securely.

Social Studies:

* History of money
* Presidents on bills
* Money around the world

Science:

* How money is made
* Coins
* Bureau of Printing and Engraving

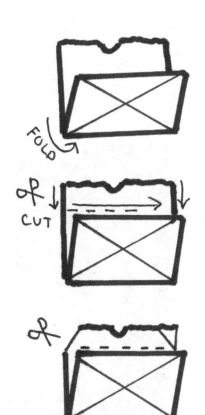

4. Open the bag up and tape the sides of the bottom flap to form a pocket.

5. At the top inside of the bag, cut the top layer angled and slightly shorter. (This will make the top pocket easier to access.)

6. Decorate the Lunch Bag Wallet and create your own money or credit cards to go inside. It's also a great place to store vocabulary or note cards.

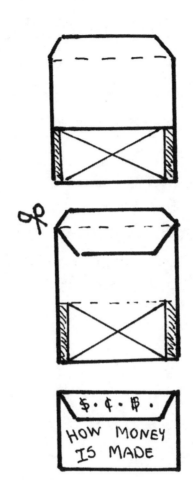

Step-n-Pocket Bag: Side One

Materials needed:

* Brown paper grocery bag
* Three envelopes
* One cheap paper plate
* 9 in. X 12 in. construction paper
  (yellow, green, blue, brown, and white)
* Blackline masters (pp. 157-159)
* Crayons, markers, or colored pencils
* Glue
* Stapler

Social Studies:

* Environments
* Plants
* Animals

Science:

* Light energy
* Heat energy
* Sound energy

Instructions:

1. Cut the construction paper to the following sizes (All pieces should be 9-inches wide and vary in length): Yellow-2 inches, green-4 inches, blue-6 inches, brown-8 inches, and white-10 inches. Lay the colors in order, from the shortest to longest on top of each other and staple to the bottom flap of the bag, creating a stepbook.

2. Color the paper plate to resemble the Earth using green and blue crayons. Glue the plate to the bottom flap of the bag. Glue a label on the world that reads, "What does my Earth have?"

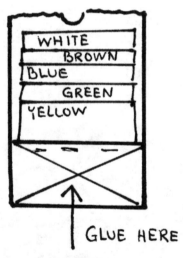

3. Use the appropriate labels, plant pictures, and animal pictures for each layer of the bag: yellow-desert; green-forest, blue-water; brown-mountains; white-Arctic and Antarctic regions. The edges of the layers can be cut to add details.

4. On the brown bag, glue a yellow circle to represent the sun. Allow it to peek out from behind the mountain tops. Characters can be added to the project if desired.

43

Step-n-Pocket Bag: Side Two
Energy Project

Materials needed:

* Brown paper grocery bag
* Three envelopes
* One cheap paper plate
* 9 in. X 12 in. construction paper
  (yellow, green, blue, brown, and white)
* Blackline masters (p. 160)
* Crayons, markers, or colored pencils
* Glue
* Stapler
* 8 1/2 in. X 11 in. white paper

Social Studies:

*Environments
*Plants
*Animals

Science:

*Light energy
*Heat energy
*Sound energy

Instructions:

1. Flip the Step-n-Pocket Bag: Side One project to the back side. Glue on blackline master for the energy project. Trace the words with crayons, markers, or colored pencils, and illustrate with simple scientific diagrams.

2. Seal each envelope and cut one edge away to make a pocket from the envelope. Glue each envelope to the bag near the energy labels.

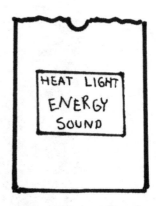

3. Using the white 8 1/2 in. X 11 in. paper, cut into small squares that will fit into each envelope and staple together to create mini-books.

4. Use each mini-book to write about different kinds of energy. They can also be used to take notes or record new vocabulary words.

* The inside of this bag can also be used to hold materials while completing this project. When finished, it can be storage for other activities that need to get home safely.

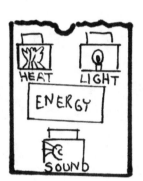

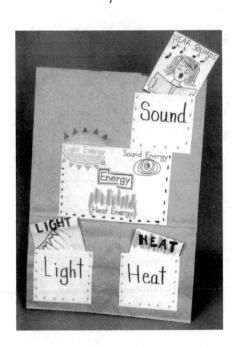

Thanksgiving Bag

Materials needed:

* Brown paper grocery bag
* Two cheap paper plates
* One brass fastener
* Stapler
* 3 in. X 6 in. sheet of brown construction paper
* Crayons, markers, or colored pencils
* Scissors
* Glue
* Blackline masters (pp. 161-162)

Social Studies:

* Giving thanks
* Pilgrims
* Indians

Science:

* Foods
* Nutrition
* Turkeys

Instructions:

1. Cut a window into the brown bag on the plain side near the opening of the bag as shown.

2. Attach a paper plate near the opening edge of the brown bag by placing the plate inside the bag and fastening with the brass fastener.

3. Enlarge the Horn-of-Plenty blackline and trace onto the bag. Decorate it and add words, "I am thankful for…" Turn and illustrate the plate.

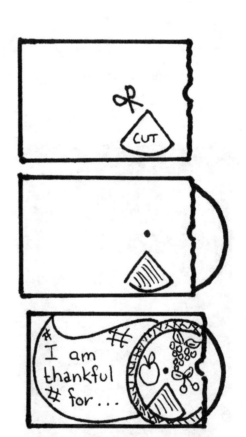

4. Flip the bag to the other side with the flap on the bottom. Staple the flap closed on each side to create a pocket.

5. Trace and cut out the turkey head from the brown construction paper. Glue the turkey head to the flap of the bag and decorate to resemble a turkey.

6. On one side of the plate draw and color turkey feathers to cover the entire plate. Flip the plate over and illustrate favorite Thanksgiving foods. Place plate in pocket when completed.

3-D Tree

Materials needed:

* Brown paper lunch bag
* Scissors
* Glue or glue stick
* Small scraps of paper

Instructions:

1. Open the brown paper lunch bag. Hold the bag from the open end and cut down all of the folded pleats to the first crease line to make strips.

2. Continue cutting strips around the bag approximately the same width. (Six cuts in the bag is a good idea.)

3. Hold the bag upside down so the strips are hanging down. Grab the bag below the flat base and twist, twist, and twist to form a trunk.

Social Studies:

* Family tree
* History
* Branches of government

Science:

* Seasons of the tree
* Parts of a tree
* Life in a tree

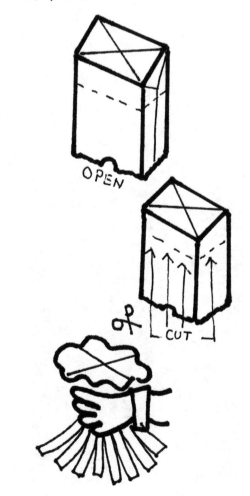

OPEN

or

CUT

4. Students may enjoy giving the base of the tree a few "slaps" to keep it flat.

5. Flip the bag over so the base is at the bottom. Take each strip and twist it individually and fairly tightly to form each branch. Be sure to twist the branches all the way to the end.

6. For some variety, you may cut the end of the branch strips to form two smaller limbs.

7. Students can attach information to the branches of the tree using the scraps of paper and glue.

49

Timeline Bag

Materials needed:

* Brown paper grocery bag
* Scissors
* Glue
* Blackline masters (pp. 163-164)
* Crayons, markers, or colored pencils
* Ruler

Social Studies:

* Famous people
* Historic events
* School year happenings

Science:

* Phases of the moon
* Astronomy
* Changes over time

Instructions:

1. Lay the bag down with the bottom flap side up and cut down the top layer of the brown bag only (cutting a vertical slit down the center of the bag, stopping at the flap). Now, cut horizontally just above the flap and to the edges of the bag.

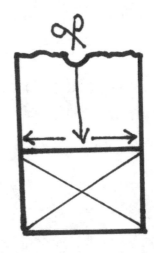

2. Flip the bag to the back side and use a marker and ruler to draw a line down the center of the bag for the timeline.

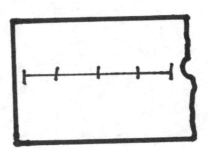

3. Use this line for the timeline. Create pictures in the blackline master boxes and glue them in order on the bag: one above the line and the next one below the line.

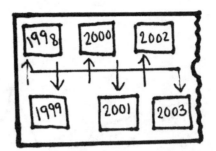

4. Flip the bag to the side with the flap and glue a label and illustration to the bottom flap of the bag. The label should relate to the topic of study, for example, the life of Martin L. King.

* Or, the illustration master (p. 164) could be labeled "I Have a Dream."

5. On each of the cut flaps at the top of the bag, write a question about your topic of study. Open the flaps to reveal the answers to the questions.

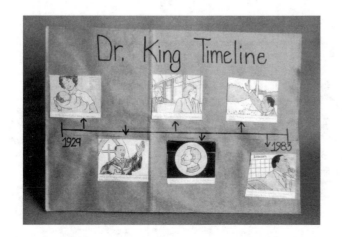

Box Projects

Boxes

Boxes, containers, many shapes and sizes
CD cases, cereal boxes, all complete with prizes,
Greeting cards make boxes,
Cassette tape holders too,
Band-Aid boxes, most teachers have a few.
Candy boxes, pizza boxes, chips cans, oh my
Sadly, the containers that I myself supply!
Match boxes, tissue boxes, small mint tins,
Keep saving these containers and
Every student wins!
We take these boxes and fill them with skills
Then we create, decorate, and fill the windowsills
With 3-D boxes that shake and roll
They hold basic facts, vocabulary, and whatever your goal
Make a box and cover it, teach skills they can see—
Hands-on learning with the result of mastery!

The Box Projects

Containers for projects

This section is called "containers for projects" because we first collected all types and sizes of containers to make our box projects. That will be your first step, too. Put labeled bins in your classroom and watch them fill up with everyday materials that will make these very special box projects, or follow our suggestions to find your own materials. First, you will need these containers:

* CD containers—the first time we decided to use these was when a friend was moving and brought us a boxful of her daughters' empty CD containers saying, "I knew The Bag Ladies would think of something to do with these." We couldn't let her down. Now, many CD projects later, we either have students bring in empty CD cases or we purchase them at discount warehouses in colored or clear containers.

* Band-Aid boxes—the paper Band-Aid boxes can be covered and used for your projects or you can obtain magnetic Band-Aid boxes from any arts and crafts catalog.
  Other magnetic boxes include: breath mint boxes (all sizes), watch boxes, and cookie tins.

* Greeting cards—save all kinds and sizes of greeting cards. These can make all sizes of boxes.

* Cereal and popcorn-size boxes—not only will these make great projects but when the students present their projects to their classmates, you can add the bowls, spoons, and milk so students can enjoy a treat while they listen to the presentation. (We find that a full mouth helps the listening process considerably!)

* Pizza boxes and other take-out boxes—try asking for free boxes at pizza restaurants rather than using used ones, but both can work.

* Chip holders—these come in great can shapes or triangular shapes for some creative projects.

* Candy boxes—you know those heart-shaped boxes you received on Valentine's Day from all of your students? These make a *sweet* project that you will *love*.

* Other containers—get creative! What other containers would make great box projects?

Tips for Making the Box Projects

Be sure that you have more than the correct number of containers. Have your model complete and ready to show to the class, and always encourage students to add their own flair to the project. Tell your students what the objective will be once the project is complete, either to have a study tool for testing or to demonstrate mastery of the topic. (Sometimes the project is used as a teaching tool for the standard, and students fill in parts of the activity along with the teacher.) The project will usually take about a week but can vary depending on your schedule. Here is a suggested way to present a project to your classes:

* After teaching the skill appropriate for the project, pass out the materials needed for Day 1. Show the model and discuss the rubric for this activity.
* Have the students work on the project for about 45 minutes. The project and the leftover materials are then collected and stored in the student bag holders for this unit. This way the students have their own projects and all materials they are using in one convenient location. This also keeps your room organized and neat.
* On Day 2, teach your regular lesson (read a piece of literature, etc). For the last 20 minutes, allow students to take out their materials from their bag holders and work on the activity quietly, again cleaning up as they did on Day 1.
* You may continue this model for the next two days or allow students to complete the project at home. It is important for them to get a good start in class so that they are comfortable with the objectives of the activity.
* For half the time, have the students present their projects in 3-minute presentations. If they do not present, collect all the projects, grade them on the rubric, and post several on the bulletin board. (Unless they are used as study guides, in which case post them after the test). Try to vary the students' posted projects so that every student gets one or more of his/her projects posted each month. Keep the other projects in the student bag holders.

Parent Communication

Using the student bag holders, we send home all tests, projects, written activities, and rubrics to be signed every other week. This procedure allows parents an open communication with you as well as the opportunity to see their child's study guides and test results. It also allows you to write to the parents any correspondence, positive or negative, that you feel necessary. The parents may then respond back to you immediately.

Band-Aid® Box

Materials needed:

* Band-Aid box (or any box approximately 3 in. X 4 in.)
* Paper large enough to cover box
* Crayons, markers, or colored pencils
* Band-Aid blackline (p. 165)
* Cellophane tape

Instructions:

1. Cover and decorate the box using paper, tape, crayons, markers or colored pencils. Label the box with words and illustrations to fit the topic.

2. Cut out the images on the blackline master and write the questions on the printed side.

3. Flip the Band-Aids over and write the answers to the questions on the back. Use the Band-Aids to "aid" you in teaching topic facts.

Social Studies:

* War and outcomes
* States and capitals
* Fact or fiction

Science:

* Rules for recycling
* Animals and babies
* Safety rules for science

Other suggestions:

* Glue the Band-Aids to card stock to make them more sturdy.

* Attach real Band-Aids to paper. Cut out. Write the questions on the front with permanent marker, then flip to the back and write the answers.

* Instead of a Band-Aid box, make a first aid kit or survival kit that relates to the topic of study.

* Other boxes that would work for this project include metal mint boxes, small jewelry boxes, or tea bag boxes.

* Small books, cassettes, and game boards can also fit into these boxes. Be creative!

Box Guitar

Materials needed:

* Shoebox with no lid
* Rubber bands of different widths
* Tempera paint (two shades of brown)
* Paintbrush with stiff bristles
* Paper towel roll
* Glue
* Scissors

Instructions:

1. Paint the paper towel roll and the entire shoebox (a few sides at a time). Let them dry.

2. Without wetting your brush, lightly brush a lighter brown color over the dark brown paint. This will make your box look like real wood. Let it dry.

3. Glue the paper towel roll to the short end of the shoebox. Allow glue to dry completely.

Social Studies:

* History of instruments
* Famous composers
* Cultural differences

Science:

* Pitch of sounds
* Create a study song
* Vibration

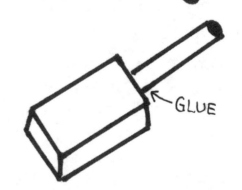

GLUE

4. Stretch the rubber bands around the open area of the shoebox. Space them out evenly, from the widest to the most narrow rubber band.

5. Experiment by plucking the strings one at a time and by strumming the strings all at once.

Other musical instrument suggestions:

* Rhythm sticks can be made from two wood dowel rods.
* Shakers can be made from paper cups, paper towel rolls, or dried gourds and filled with rice, beans or small beads.
* Drums can be made from a coffee can or oatmeal can with a lid.
* Tambourines can be made from paper plates and jingle bells by hole-punching along the edges of a paper plate and attaching the jingle bells.

* Having a contest to see who can be the most creative and design a unique musical instrument is always fun for everyone!

Brown-Bag Box

Materials needed:

* Brown paper bag (any size)
* Scissors
* Crayons, markers, or colored pencils
* 1 in. square of sticky-back Velcro®
* Two brass paper fasteners

Social Studies:

* Vacation treasures
* Pirate treasure box
* Things I treasure

Science:

* Precious minerals
* Nutritious recipes box
* Underground finds

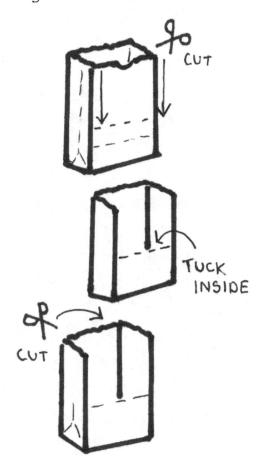

Instructions:

1. Open bag up and cut down the front two edges to the first crease.

2. Gently fold the front side of the bag inside and across the bottom of the bag. This will give your box more support.

3. Next, cut down the back two edges in the same way you did the front but do not tuck them inside.

4. Cut the tops off the side panels about 2 to 3 inches above the crease. Round the edges off.

5. To close your box securely, either roll the back panel forward and tuck inside the box approximately 1 inch or attach a piece of sticky-back Velcro® to the outside.

6. Decorate your box with crayons, markers, or colored pencils. A handle can also be added by attaching the scraps from the bag with brass fasteners.

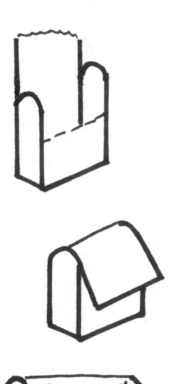

THINGS I TREASURE

Tools for Plant RESEARCH

Candy-Box Accordion Book

Materials needed:

* Candy box (the kind chocolate candy comes in)
* Paper to cover box
* 8 1/2 in. X 11 in. paper (several sheets)
* Glue stick
* Cellophane tape
* Scissors
* Crayons, markers, or colored pencils
* Ruler

Instructions:

1. Cover the candy box with paper and cut the paper to fit the front and back. Glue the paper into place with the glue stick.

2. Decorate the front and back of the box according to your unit topic using the crayons, markers, and colored pencils.

Social Studies:

* Timelines
* Portraits of presidents
* Compare and contrast

Science:

* Sequence of an experiment
* Life cycles
* Record a collection

3. Measure the box to determine the size of the accordion book that will fit inside: It's best to subtract about a half-inch both vertically and horizontally.

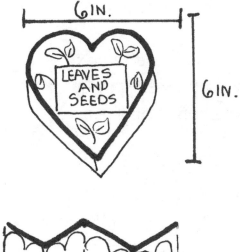

4. Fold the 8 1/2 in. X 11 in. paper accordion-style to fit the dimensions of the box. Cut the paper to fit inside. To make a longer book, repeat with several more sheets of paper.

5. Tape the sheets of paper together, and write about the unit topic on each page. When book is complete, rub glue stick in the bottom of the box and place book inside.

Cassette-Box Seed Starter

Materials needed:

* Empty cassette box
* Compressed sponge or
  kitchen sponge
* Pencil
* Hole puncher
* Fine-tip black marker
* Sticky-back blank label
* Easy-to-germinate seeds

Instructions:

1. To speed germination of the
seeds, soak the seeds in a cup
of water for about three
hours.

2. Cut the sponge into a
2 1/2 in. X 4 in. rectangle.
Open the cassette box. Rub
the pencil over the post
points on the inside. Place the
sponge in the cassette tape
box and gently close the box.
The pencil lead will mark the
placement of the posts.

Social Studies:

* Where seeds grow
* Mapping seed growth
* Johnny Appleseed

Science:

* Seed starter
* Label seed parts
* Measure seed growth

3. Remove the sponge from the case and hole punch on the pencil marks.

4. Dampen the sponge, then place both the sponge and seeds into the cassette box.

5. Use the fine-tip black marker and sticky-back label to label the seed starter with your name, date, and kind of seed you planted.

6. Watch your seeds grow! When large enough, transplant the seeds into the ground or flower pot.

* The Bag Ladies also like to use cassette boxes as storage boxes for small game pieces, manipulatives, and Button Bugs.

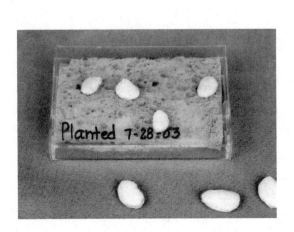

Cereal Box

Materials needed:

* Cereal Box
* Blackline master (pp. 166-167)
* Scissors
* Crayons, markers, or colored pencils
* Glue
* Supplies to serve cereal with milk

Instructions:

1. Using the blackline master, choose an American hero or scientist to illustrate on the cover of the box. Draw with pencil, outline with black marker, color, and add a background.

2. Tell a story about the hero or scientist on the other part of the blackline. Who are they? Why are they remembered? Add other important facts.

Social Studies:

* American heroes
* Folk heroes
* Immigrants

Science:

* Inventories
* Scientists
* Student scientists

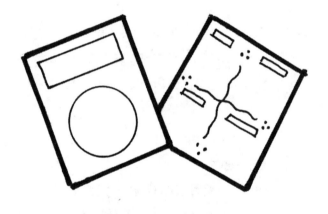

MY HERO

3. The side panels can be used to compare yourself to the person you research or to add additional information that relates to your topic.

4. Remove the cereal bag from the inside. Cut out and glue the blackline onto the cereal box. In small groups, students give their oral reports and share the cereal and milk.

5. After the boxes are completed and presentations have been given, cut the box open down one side, and hang up the flat boxes for display.

* Sometimes we put student-made games and puzzles on the inside of the box. It's like finding a prize in a box of cereal!

CD Accordion Book

Materials needed:

* Empty CD cases
* Blackline master (p. 168)
* Glue or cellophane tape
* Crayons, markers, or colored pencils
* 4 1/2 in. X 4 1/2 in. piece of card stock
* Scissors

Instructions:

1. Cut out the desired number of CDs from the blackline master in pairs that overlap. Remember to cut the center hole out from each CD so they will fit into the case. Glue or tape the tabs together to form a "string" of CDs.

2. Create illustrations, outline in marker, and color on the CDs to match the objective. Make sure the CDs follow a sequential order from left to right.

Social Studies:

* Continent research
* Political debate
* Oceans of the world

Science:

* Vocabulary book
* Scientific procedures
* States of matter

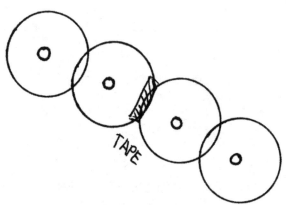

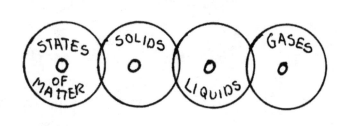

3. Start with the first picture and fold the CDs to form an accordion-style booklet.

4. Lay the booklet inside the CD case so that by pulling on the top CD the booklet will unfold in sequential order.

5. Design and illustrate a cover or title page on the card stock square that shows the topic of study in the CD "story."

CD Journal

Materials needed:

* Empty CD case
* 8 1/4 in. X 4 1/4 in. white paper
* 8 1/2 in. X 4 1/2 in. construction paper
* Crayons, markers, or colored pencils
* Long-armed stapler

Social Studies:

* Geography of a state
* Climates of the world
* Waterways

Science:

* Parts of a cell
* Life cycles
* Scientific process

Instructions:

1. Carefully empty the CD case by popping out the cardboard or plastic insert.

2. Place the 8 1/2 in. X 4 1/2 in. construction paper under the white paper and fold them in half horizontally.

3. Staple the paper together on the horizontal fold line, then refold.

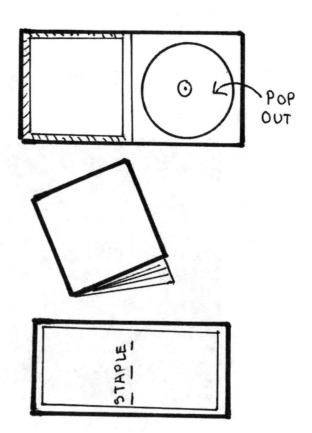

4. Design a cover for your CD-case journal that goes along with the topic of study.

5. On each page of the inside, write the most important information from the unit. Create illustrations and color.

6. Place your journal inside the CD case for safe storage. A small pen or pencil can also be placed inside the case to use when writing in the journal.

* Ask the students to bring in old CD cases from home. (Many people now store their CDs in CD wallets or cases and have no use for the plastic cases.) You also can buy the cases in large quantities at wholesale clubs or office supply stores.

Coffee Can Game

Materials needed:

* Coffee can
* Construction paper
* Crayons, markers, or colored pencils
* Glue stick
* Brass paper fastener
* Small paper clip
* One 10 in. square of tagboard
* Cellophane tape
* Scissors

Instructions:

1. Cut a piece of construction paper to fit around the outside of the coffee can. Decorate the can to match the topic of your game.

2. Tape the decorated construction paper around the outside of the coffee can.

3. Using the lid of the coffee can, trace a circle onto a piece of construction paper. Divide the circle into equal sections, and put a number in each section.

Social Studies:

* Historical figure game
* Transportation game
* History of space travel

Science:

* Human body game
* Rocket launch game
* Ocean voyage game

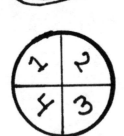

4. Push the brass fastener through the center of the lid and secure. Add a paper clip to the fastener to create the spinner for your game.

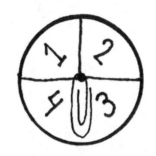

5. Create a game board using the 10 in. square of tagboard. It is helpful to look at some simple game boards first before trying to create your own.

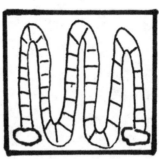

6. Write a set of rules and objectives for your game. Store the game board, game pieces, and other pieces for the game inside the coffee can. Have fun trying to play each other's games.

Collections in a Box

Materials needed:

* Shoebox or box of similar size
* 10 zipper-style baggies
* Clear, wide packaging tape
* Wrapping paper to cover box
* Scissors
* 10 sticky labels
* 4 in. X 4 in. square of paper
* Glue stick

Social Studies:

* Stamp collection
* Postcard collection
* Flags of the world

Science:

* Leaf collection
* Soil samples
* Wildflower collection

Instructions:

1. Cover the outside of the box with the wrapping paper. Wrap the box's top and bottom separately like a gift with a removable lid.

2. Create a label from the 4 in. X 4 in. paper that says "MY COLLECTION," and your name. Glue label to the box lid.

3. Using the clear, wide packaging tape, lay two zipper bags out side-by-side and tape the vertical edges together. Continue this with all 10 zipper bags.

4. Fold the bags back and forth like an accordion.

5. Tape the bottom bag to the bottom of the box. Fold all the other bags accordion-style and place the lid on top.

6. You are now ready to start your collection. As you collect things, open a zipper bag and label them with a sticky label.

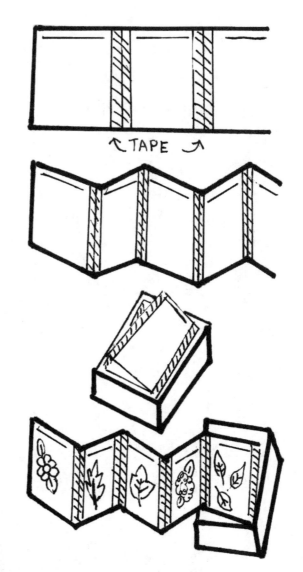

A Different Diorama

Materials needed:

* One legal-size file folder
* One standard manila file folder
* Assorted scraps of construction paper
* Crayons, markers, or colored pencils
* Scissors
* Stapler
* Glue stick
* Ruler

Instructions:

1. Cut the tab of both folders so the edges of the folders are even.

2. Cut both folders in half on the center fold line. You will only use half of each folder to create this project.

3. Lay the legal-size folder piece horizontally and create a scene or background to go along with your topic or theme.

Social Studies:

* Scene from history
* Travel scene
* My community

Science:

* Environmental scene
* Dinosaur scene
* Wild weather scene

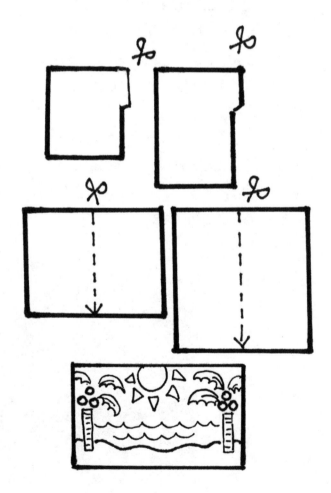

4. Using the standard-size folder piece, measure and cut out the center to create a frame.

5. Place the frame on top of the diorama background and staple along one vertical edge.

6. Match up the other vertical edges of the frame to the background, so that the background takes on a three-dimensional effect.

7. Using the scraps of paper, create people, plants, and animals to be part of your scene. Cut out and glue them into place on your diorama.

STAPLE

HOUGHTON MIFFLIN HARCOURT

East Regional Office
151 Benigno Boulevard
Bellmawr, NJ 08031
sales support 800-426-6577
sales support fax 800-277-4707

Nancy Quinn
Pennsylvania
Sales Representative
mobile 267-981-5363
office 215-343-2668
nancyquinn@hmhpub.com
www.hmhpub.com

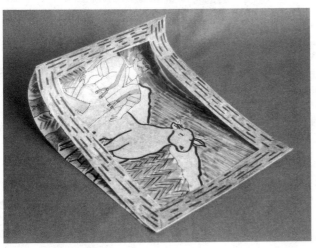

Food Box Suitcase

Materials needed:

* Empty food box, about the size of a cereal box
* 8 1/2 in. X 11 in. construction paper
* Four brass paper fasteners
* Blackline masters (pp. 169-170)
* Ribbon
* Scissors
* Tape
* Hole puncher
* Glue stick

Social Studies:

* Study a country
* Foods of the world
* World cultures

Science:

* Name the scientist
* Science experiment case
* Invention box

Instructions:

1. Tape the box closed around the edges. Make a lid on one side of the box by cutting a slit 3/4 in. from three of the edges, then down both sides to the end of the box.

2. Using the hole puncher, attach brass fasteners to the lid and to the side of the box along the longest edge. Tie a ribbon onto one of the brass fasteners, twist the ribbon around the other brass fastener to secure the suitcase lid.

3. Fold a piece of construction paper accordion-style to form a handle 8 1/2 in. long. Insert brass fasteners into each end of the handle and attach to the side of the box.

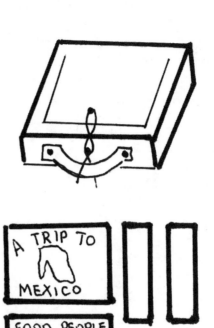

4. Cut out blackline masters, decorate and label with information to go along with theme or unit of study. Glue the blackline masters to the suitcase. (Sides can also be covered with scraps of construction paper.)

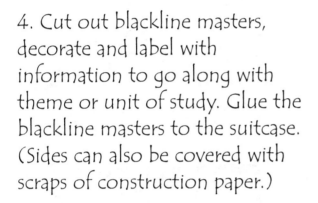

5. Store projects, notes and other important theme or unit information inside suitcase.

Greeting Card Box

Materials needed:

* Greeting cards
  (various sizes and types)
* Scissors
* Tape

Social Studies:

* Vocabulary card storage
* Fact cards
* Stamp collection

Science:

* Shake-n-guess boxes
* Measurement
* Estimating box

Instructions:

1. Cut a greeting card along fold and separate front of card from the inside message piece.

2. Using message piece of the card, cut away 1/4 in. from the length and width.

3. Fold message piece of card in half lengthwise, then unfold.

4. Fold each lengthwise side of the card to the center fold line. We call this a "double-door" fold.

5. Measure to the first crease and fold the top and bottom of the message piece in equal amounts.

6. Repeat steps 4 and 5 with the front of the card. On both pieces of the card, cut four slits as shown.

7. Form a box by tucking the double-folded ends under and taping them inside the box.

8. Your box is now ready to hold small items that go along with your topic of study or unit.

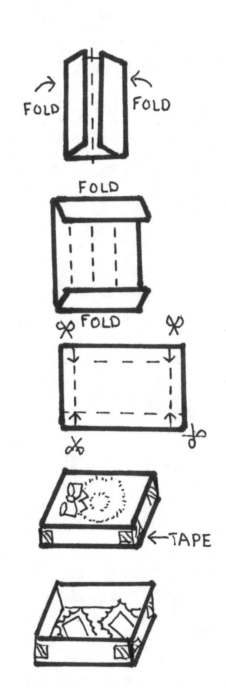

Greeting Card Display Box

Materials needed:

* Greeting cards of various
  sizes and types
* Scraps of clear plastic
  (like those from a
  laminating machine)
* Scissors
* Tape

Social Studies:

* Coins of the world
* Artifacts
* State symbols

Science:

* Shell collection
* Seed samples
* Rocks

Instructions:

1. Cut a greeting card along
fold and separate front of card
from the inside.

2. Using message piece of the
card, cut away 1/4 in. from
the length and width.

3. Start by folding the inside
piece of card first. Fold
message piece of card in half
lengthwise, then unfold.

4. Fold each lengthwise side of the card to the center fold line. We call this a "double-door" fold.

5. Measure to the first crease and fold the top and bottom of the card the same amount.

6. Repeat steps 4 and 5 with the front of the card. Once the card is folded, cut a square window out of the center of the card and tape plastic into place from back side.

7. On both pieces of the card, cut four slits, tuck and tape to create a box. Use these boxes to display collectibles that go along with topic or unit of study.

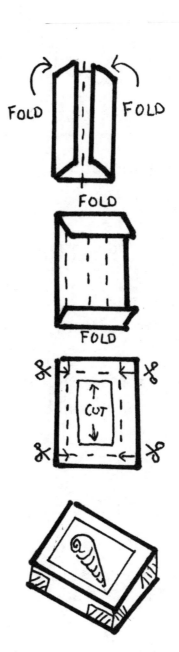

Magnetic Boxes

Materials needed:

* Magnetic tins (mint, cookie, or Band-Aid)
* Old magazines and newspapers
* Scissors
* Tagboard (large enough to cover lid of tin)
* Two-sided tape
* Crayons, markers, or colored pencils
* Sticky-back magnetic strip or business-card magnets

Social Studies:

* Matching games
* State/Capitals
* Create a poem

Science:

* Chemical formulas
* Animal kingdoms
* Create a poem

Instructions:

1. Cut words and pictures from magazines or newspapers that go with theme or unit of study.

2. Attach each word or picture to a piece of sticky-back magnet.

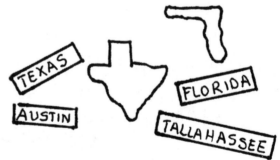

3. Using the tagboard, two-sided tape, crayons, markers, or colored pencils, make a decorative cover for the tin to match the theme or unit of study.

4. Use the magnet words and pictures on the inside of the tin to create stories and poems that go along with the topic of study.

* This can be an on-going project that can be added to throughout the school year. The students can also draw their own pictures, use clip art from the computer, or type their own words. The magnet does not need to cover the entire back side of the pictures or words—to save money, you can glue the pictures and words to tagboard and place a small piece of magnet on back of each.

Match Box Project

Materials needed:

* Empty match box
* Sticky-back craft foam scraps
* Glue
* Scissors
* Pipe cleaner
* Scraps of paper
* Crayons, markers, or colored pencils

Instructions:

1. Cut craft foam to cover the match box on all sides.

2. Glue craft foam pieces onto outside of match box. Decorate with additional craft foam scraps.

3. Use paper scraps to design inside items such as: mini-book, animal-track matching game, flash cards, or postage stamps.

Social Studies:

* Mini-book on any topic
* Design a postage stamp
* Trouble-doll box

Science:

* Mini-book on any topic
* Matching card game
* Animal-track matching

4. Use the pipe cleaner to create trouble dolls. Cut a 4-inch piece of pipe cleaner, fold in half, and twist twice.

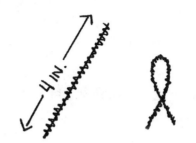

5. Cut a piece of pipe cleaner 2 inches long and twist around the center of the 4-inch piece to form the arms. Repeat this process for additional dolls.

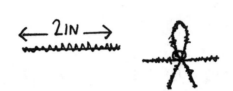

* Trouble dolls are also called worry dolls. People in some cultures place them under a pillow at night to collect the day's troubles. By morning, all troubles or worries are gone! Keep them in a match box until needed.

Pizza Box Game Board

Materials needed:

* Pizza box or box of similar style
* Crayons, markers, or colored pencils
* Brass paper fastener
* Glue stick
* Scissors
* Paper clip
* Scrap paper
* Blackline masters (pp. 171–172)

Instructions:

1. Create a game using the skills learned in a unit of study. Create a spinner on the lid of the pizza box with the scrap paper, brass fastener, and paper clip.

2. Write directions and design playing cards for the game. Add them to the pizza box lid.

3. Use the blackline masters to design the actual playing board in the box bottom or create it on a piece of paper, then glue it inside the pizza-box bottom.

Social Studies:

* Explorer game
* Civil War timeline game
* Classroom cooperation game

Science:

* Weather game
* Space travel game
* Time travel game

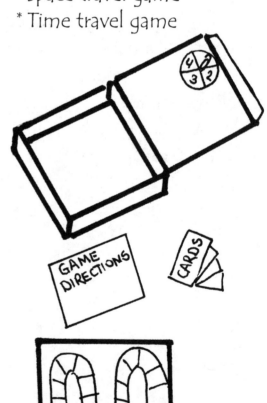

4. Name your game and create an attractive design for the cover of the box.

5. It may be necessary to include the answers to the playing-card questions to assist those playing the game.

* We find it helpful to first design a rough draft for the game board. If you cannot think of a game board design, look at commercially designed games. These game boards will help design a pathway before adding game details.

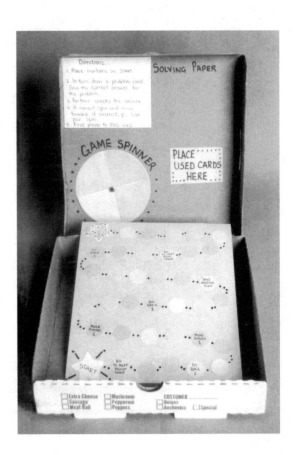

Take-Out Container Box

Materials needed:

* Cardstock paper
  8 1/2 in. X 11 in.
* Soft wire
* Tape
* Glue stick
* Scissors
* Blackline masters
  (pp. 173-174)

Social Studies:

* Research an ancient
  civilization
* Field trip finds
* Build a historical scene

Science:

* Collect bugs
* Create an environment
* Create a collection

Instructions:

1. Cut out the take-out
container from the
blacklines and glue onto
card stock.

2. Fold on the dotted lines
and glue together at the
tabs to form a container.

3. Add wire to form a handle.

4. Scenes can be built inside the container using details learned from the topic or unit of study.

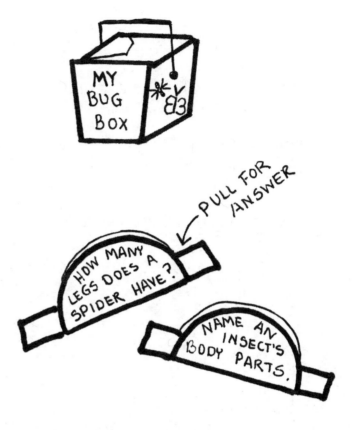

5. The outside of the container can also be decorated to match a topic. Then use brown paper to make fortune cookies and place them inside the container. The cookies' "fortunes" can be the topic facts or questions that need to be answered.

Tennis Ball Tube

Materials needed:

* Clear tennis ball tube with lid
* Masking tape
* Construction paper scraps
* Tag board scraps
* String
* Crayons, markers, or colored pencils
* Pipe cleaners
* Glue

Social Studies:

* Time capsule
* Historic diorama
* Ship in a bottle

Science:

* Environmental diorama
* Aquarium
* Planets

Instructions:

1. Choose a topic for the Tennis Ball Tube project. For example, "An Explorer's Ship in a Bottle" or "My Aquarium."

2. Decide what objects best illustrate the topic. Next, create items to be placed inside the tube to form a scene about the topic.

3. Glue or hang the items inside the tube.

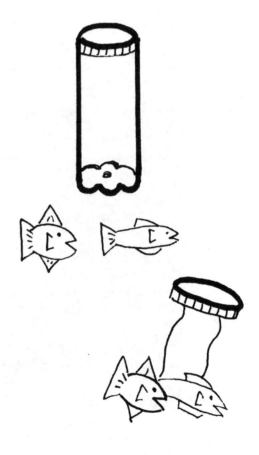

4. After the scene has been created, place the lid on the tube and label it as if it were part of a museum exhibit.

5. As an extension to this activity, write a narrative or fictional piece about the scene inside the tube.

* Be creative and use items like cotton, ice cream sticks, sand, dirt, silk flowers, glitter, sequins, and fabric scraps to make your scene come alive inside the tube. When using these items to create your scene, it's helpful to use a cool-melt glue gun to secure them into place.

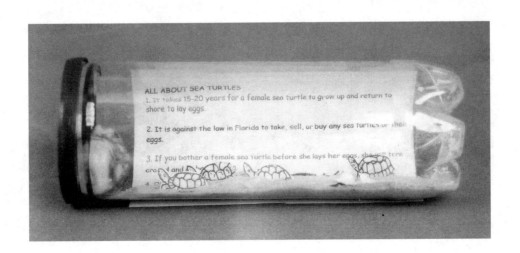

Triangle Chip Box

Materials needed:

* Three-sided chip container or any other can with plastic top
* Construction paper 9 in. X 12 in.
* Crayons, markers, or colored pencils
* Glue stick
* Ten 3 in. X 5 in. index cards
* Scissors
* Tape

Instructions:

1. Cover the three-sided container with construction paper. Cut and tape paper to fit around the container.

2. Write three different topics or titles around the three sides of the container. Example: Fact-Opinion-Fantasy; Beginning-Middle-End; or Solid-Liquid-Gas.

Social Studies:

* Beginning-middle-end of a story
* Eras in history
* Fact-Opinion-Fantasy

Science:

* States of matter
* Layers of the Earth
* Scientific classifications

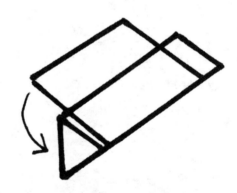

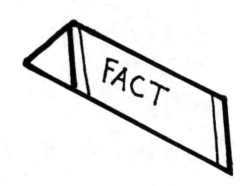

3. Cut the 10 index cards in half vertically, so you have twenty 5 in. X 1 1/2 in. cards.

4. Write examples of each of the three topics around the outside of the container. Place cards inside container.

5. Exchange containers with another person to see if they can match the cards inside the container to the topics on the outside. Example: Once upon a time-story beginning; Water vapor-gas; or I like ice cream-opinion.

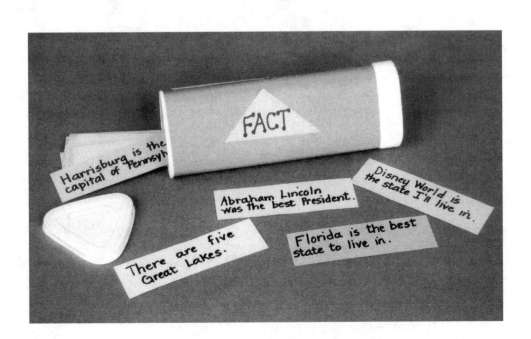

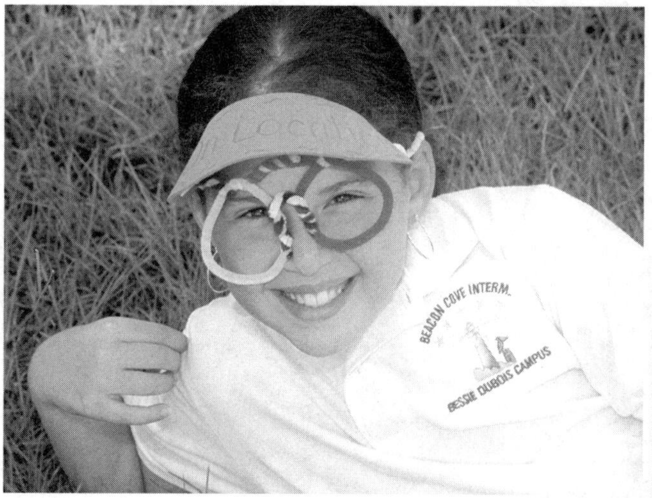
BEACON COVE INTERM.
BESSIE DUBOIS CAMPUS

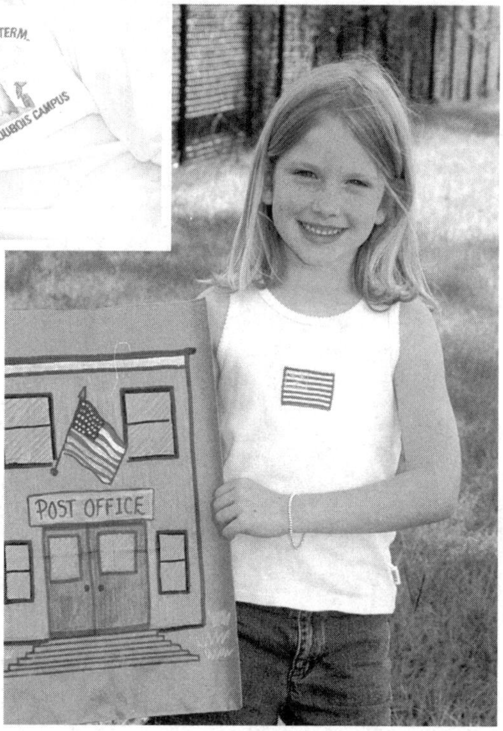
POST OFFICE

Buttons and Beyond Projects

Buttons

I never knew all the things that a button could be,
Counters, or symbols, or an old memory.
Closings on pouches, or leaves on a tree,
I never knew all the things that a button could be.

Buttons are bugs, or can slide on a string—
They make a necklace or even a ring.
Buttons make people or toys that are great.
Buttons make stamps used to decorate.

I never knew all the things that a button could do
But I don't question something that's helping me teach you.

Buttons and Beyond

Buttons? Why buttons?

Whether you are sorting button bugs by size in the primary grades or using them to remind you of outfits worn on special days, buttons are a great item for learning activities. Buttons can be purchased in large assorted containers, or students delight in bringing in unique and interesting buttons of all sorts! Besides the projects, they make great faux closings when glued onto pouch holders and can be used to decorate other bag holders and projects. Continue to add to your button collection throughout the year.

Beyond…

We will use many other items in this section of the book that motivate students to apply the standards in new ways. We keep these supplies in labeled, stackable storage bins for easy access.

Other materials used and suggested places to find them:

* Envelopes—all sizes and shapes. Check with card stores after major holidays for leftover envelopes that they will donate.
* Sample fabric rectangles—pull out of upholstery books donated from fabric shops.
* Cheap paper plates
* Film canisters—black or clear with tops. Ask any film processing center to save them for you. We leave a bag at the center for easy collection and pick up.
* File folders—manila and colored folders can be used and recycled.
* Denim pockets—these are hopefully old pockets from outgrown jeans.
* Calendar tubes/paper towel rolls
* Magazine pictures—these are best if collected from children's magazines or travel magazines.
* Corks—ask a wine bar to save the corks for you.
* Index cards—all sizes, white or colored
* Pony beads—all colors
* Plastic cording—the kind we used at camp, all colors.
* Eye screws—these are the tiny screws used on the backs of picture frames to attach wire. They are sold in packages of varying amounts.

* Feathers
* Fun foam—this comes in full sheets of all colors, shapes and sizes in containers with self-sticking backings.
* Adding machine paper
* Ribbon
* Ice cream sticks

Getting ready for the project days

When we plan a unit, we have already collected the materials to be used, run off the blacklines, and made all the models. We keep the entire unit together in a bin that includes an accordion folder containing manila folders for each project model, vocabulary, literature to be used with the lessons, assessments, and any other materials for that unit. We usually try to write a 3-4 week outline of our plans. As we progress through the unit, the materials are cut and ready to be passed to each student. At the end of each lesson, the models are returned to the folders for use the next year. Usually, we add one student-produced project each year to our model collection. Ask for volunteer donors.

Book-on-a-String

Materials needed:

* 1 yard leather or plastic cord
* Scissors
* Hole puncher
* 4 in. X 2 in. rectangle
* Stapler
* 4 1/2 in X 2 1/2 in.
* Assorted beads

Instructions:

1. Stack the 4 in. X 2 in. paper on top of the card stock. Fold in half like a book.

2. Open the book and staple at the fold line.

3. Hole punch (near the stapled center) through all layers of the book.

Social Studies:

* Book of lists—Presidents
* Important dates
* States and capitals

Science:

* Book of lists—classification
* Formulas
* Conversions—standard to metric measurement

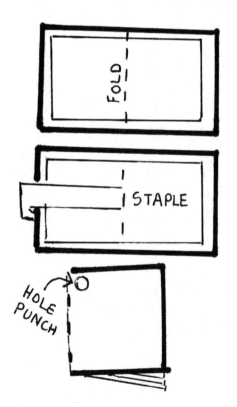

4. Lace cord through the hole and add beads to decorate the string. Tie and wear as a book necklace.

5. Book-on-a-String can be worn and written in throughout a unit of study.

* Variations: Book-on-a-String can be made into different shapes and sizes. For example, a round book can be made to look like a gold medal; a heart-shaped book can be used to write health facts in about the heart; or die-cut shapes can be cut and glued to the front cover for various topics.

Book with Wings

Materials needed:

* One sheet of unlined paper any size
* Crayons, markers, or colored pencils
* Scissors

Instructions:

1. Fold a sheet of paper vertically. Open the sheet so it falls as a tent in front of you.

2. Fold the right-hand side over to the fold in the middle. Fold the left-hand side to the fold in the middle, like a fan.

3. Open the sheet and grab it by the middle fold. As you move it up and down, it looks like a bird flying.

Social Studies:

* Political cartoons
* Maps
* Charts and graphs

Science:

* Metamorphosis
* Photosynthesis
* Frog life cycle

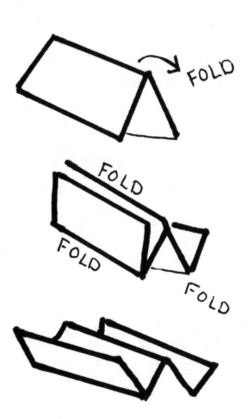

4. Using scissors, cut a slit in the middle of the folded edge to the first fold line.

5. Hold the paper on each side of the slit and pull the paper down. As the slit opens it will form a four-page booklet.

6. Crease the two folded edges at the top. Close the booklet. Use one of the top fold pages to form the cover.

7. Address the main idea of the unit on the cover. Each of the next pages will have either illustrations or written summaries about the main ideas of the lesson.

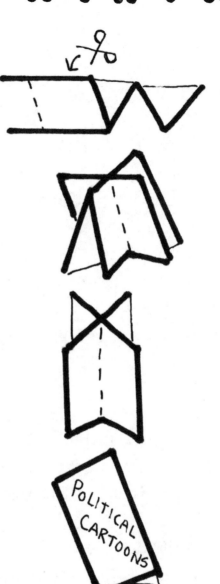

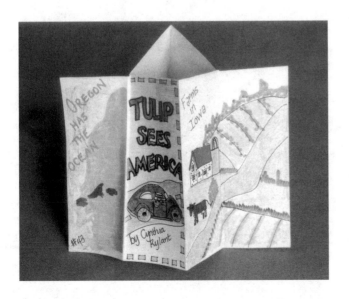

Button Bugs

Materials needed:

* Large buttons with at least two holes
* 2-3 pieces of pipe cleaner (assorted colors)
* An empty plastic cassette case
* Permanent markers in assorted colors

Instructions:

1. Put one end of the pipe cleaner into one button hole and out another button hole.

2. Twist the ends of the pipe cleaner to look like antennas.

3. Use the permanent markers to decorate the Button Bugs.

4. Store the Button Bugs in the empty plastic cassette box.

Social Studies:

* Where bugs live
* Bug rewards
* Bingo bugs

Science:

* Create a bug
* Ladybugs
* Beetles

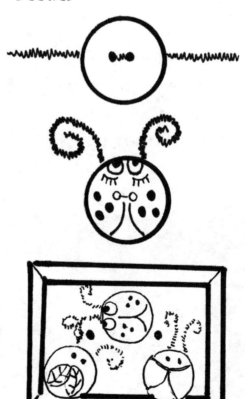

Ways to use Button Bugs:

* Where bugs live-Draw a bug's environment, add sticky-back magnets to the picture and to the back of the Button Bug. Attach the Button Bug to its environment (great activity for teaching camouflaging).

* Bug rewards-Use Button Bugs as rewards. (Students can store their bugs in a cassette case.)

* Bingo bugs-Use the Button Bugs as markers for Bingo games or any other board game.

Button Memory String

Materials needed:

* One pipe cleaner, any color
* Six to ten large, colorful
  buttons

Social Studies:

* History of the abacus
* Button colors represent unit
  concepts
* Personal history

Science:

* Patterns
* Sorting
* Button colors represent
  unit concepts

Instructions:

1. Twist the end of the pipe
cleaner around a finger to
form a loop. Twist the ends
of the pipe cleaner around
each other to secure.

2. Lace buttons onto the
pipe cleaner.

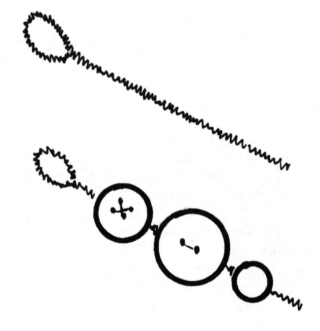

Suggested uses:

* Button Abacus—Use the buttons as an abacus. Move the buttons together or apart to add or subtract. You could also read and learn about the history of the abacus and where it was invented.

* Button colors may represent unit concepts. For example, the colors may represent the colors of a country's flag. In science, the colors of the buttons could represent the colors of the rainbow.

* Each button on the memory string can represent a student's personal history. Buttons can be collected to represent a timeline of important events in his/her life.

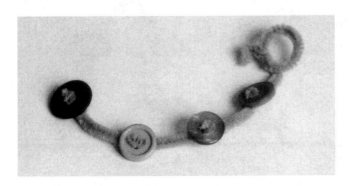

Button People

Materials needed:

* Three pipe cleaners: use tan, brown, black, yellow, or red
* Thirty 2-4 holed buttons, small to medium in size
* One 1/2 in. diameter wooden bead
* Four to six shank-style buttons: 4 matching and 2 decorative
* Ruler
* Scissors

Social Studies:

* Historical figures
* Colonial toys
* Button history

Science:

* Categorizing
* Sorting buttons
* Role playing

Instructions:

1. Measure two 7-inch pieces of pipe cleaner. Twist one shank-style button to the ends for feet.

2. Measure 3 inches on both pipe cleaners. Twist pipe cleaners together and begin stringing buttons from largest to smallest. Stack approximately ten buttons. This will form the button person's body.

3. Cut a 4-inch piece of pipe cleaner, fold in half, and twist around the top of the button stack.

4. String approximately ten buttons of equal size down each pipe cleaner to form the arms. Add a small shank-style button on the ends of the pipe cleaner to form the hands.

5. Cut another 4-inch piece of pipe cleaner and twist it around the remaining pipe cleaner that was used to create the body. String these four pieces through the wooden head bead. Curl each piece to form the hair. For shorter hair, cut the pieces.

6. For a boy-button person, buttons can be strung on the legs to resemble pants.

7. Adorn the hair or hands with decorative shank-style buttons.

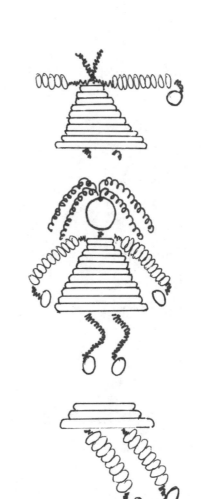

111

Button Stamps

Materials needed:

* Corks of any size or shape
* Various decorative, shank-style buttons
* Glue
* Eye screw
* 1 yard plastic lacing or ribbon
* Assorted buttons
* Assorted beads

Instructions:

1. Choose a shank-style button with a design.

2. Stand the cork on a flat end. Put a small amount of glue on top end and push the shank of button into cork. Allow glue to dry overnight.

3. Add eye screw to flat bottom end of cork by twisting the eye screw into the cork.

Social Studies:

* Portraits with button shirts
* Quilt pattern designs
* Design stationery

Science:

* Patterning
* Decorate bag holders
* Create animal bodies

4. String lacing or ribbon through the eye screw.

5. Add assorted buttons to each side of the cork. Beads can be laced between the buttons for spacing.

To stamp with the Button Stamps:

1. Use colored stamp pads or a small amount of tempera paint on a sponge.

2. Lightly press the Button Stamp into the paint and stamp onto project.

3. Crayons, markers, or colored pencils can be used to turn the stamp marks into animals, flowers, or other creations.

Camera-Shaped Book

Materials needed:

* Camera and snapshot
  blacklines (see pp. 175-176)
* 1 yard survey tape
* Hole Puncher
* Two pipe cleaners
* Crayons, markers, or colored
  pencils

Instructions:

1. Cut out the camera
blackline, which may be run
off on colored card stock,
colored copy paper, or white
paper. Carefully cut around
the flashbulb and stand bulb
up. Fold in half along the
center line.

2. Cut out the snapshots and
slip them into the camera.

3. Hole-punch through the
camera and the snapshots.

Social Studies:

* Long ago lands
* Long ago people
* Explorers

Science:

* From seed to plant
* Solids, liquids, gases
* Microscope drawings

4. Cut the pipe cleaner in half and insert one half into each hole at the top of the camera. Twist each pipe cleaner to form a loop.

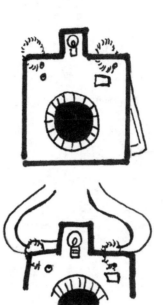

5. Insert the survey tape through the loops and tie it to make a neck strap.

6. On the snapshot blacklines, illustrate things learned about in your unit of study. Below each picture, write about the snapshot. If more room for writing is needed, continue on the back side of the snapshot.

7. The outside of the camera may be decorated, adding titles that go with unit.

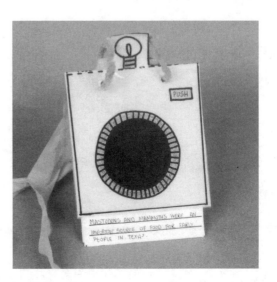

Color-Coded Bracelets

Materials needed:

* One black pipe cleaner
* Assorted colors of pony beads

Social Studies:

* Environments of the Earth
* Branches of government
* State symbols

Science:

* Water cycle
* Plant parts
* Life cycles

Instructions:

1. Twist one end of the pipe cleaner around your finger to form a loop.

2. String each bead on to form an order or sequence. Here are some examples:

The water cycle:
yellow bead = sun
white bead   = clouds
clear bead   = evaporation
blue bead   = water (lakes, oceans)
green bead   = land

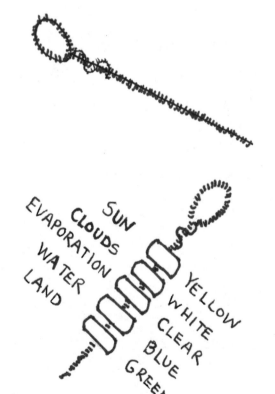

Environments of the Earth:

white bead	=	arctic regions
brown bead	=	desert regions
blue bead	=	oceans
green bead	=	rainforests
tan bead	=	mountain regions

Parts of a plant:

white bead	=	roots
light green bead	=	sprout
med. green bead	=	stalk
dark green bead	=	leaves
pink bead	=	blossom
red bead	=	flower

3. Loop bracelet around wrist. Students can use it to help remember important concepts of a lesson.

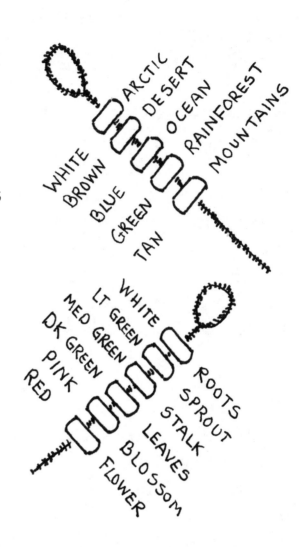

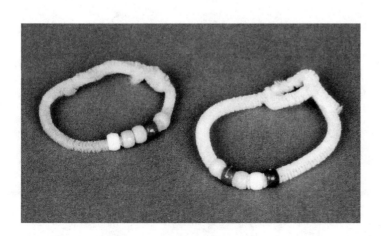

Container Necklaces

Materials needed:

* Small eye screw
* Film canister or other small plastic container with lid
* 32-36 inches plastic lacing
* Three pony beads (assorted colors)
* 2-3 feet of rolled accounting paper (width to fit container)
* Blank sticky-back label

Social Studies:

* European explorers
* Map-making
* Timelines

Science:

* Timelines
* Measuring tape
* Plants/seeds

Instructions:

1. Twist the eye screw into the lid of the film canister. If it is difficult to poke through, use something sharp to start the hole and then put the eye screw through the hole.

2. Thread the plastic lacing through the eye screw and string beads through both pieces of lacing at the same time.

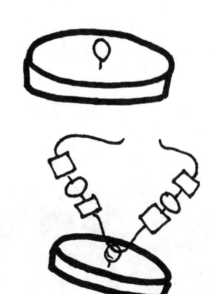

3. Roll the accounting tape inside the container and use it to record timelines, explorers, or as a measuring tape.

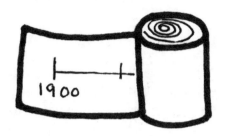

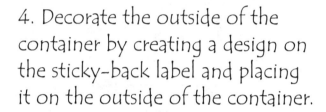

4. Decorate the outside of the container by creating a design on the sticky-back label and placing it on the outside of the container.

* To plant seeds inside the container, use a clear or opaque container. Place a damp piece of cotton inside container, along with selected seed. Put the lid on the container and wear necklace for a few days. Your seed will soon begin to sprout and grow.

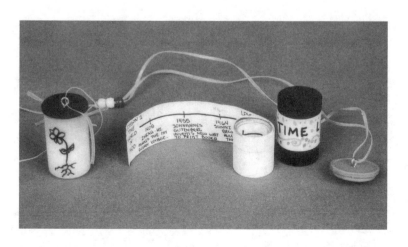

Cork Animals: Frog or Toad

Materials needed:

* One long, thin cork
* Two brown or green pipe cleaners
  (green-frog, brown-toad)
* Two wiggle eyes
* Glue
* 1 yard plastic lacing

Instructions:

1. Fold one pipe cleaner in half, wrap the pipe cleaner around the end of the cork and twist it together.

2. Bend the remaining piece of pipe cleaner into the shape of a frog's or toad's hind legs.

3. Cut the second pipe cleaner into thirds. Use two pieces to form the front legs. Slip one piece of pipe cleaner under each side of the cork to form the front legs. Bend them into position.

4. Glue wiggle eyes in front of legs. Slip lacing under pipe cleaner for necklace.

Social Studies:

* State animals
* Amphibians of a region
* Forest inhabitants

Science:

* Types of frogs
* Types of toads
* Compare frogs/toads

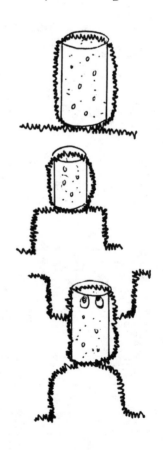

Cork Animals: Owl or Bird

Materials needed:

* One long, thin cork
* One medium-size orange or brown pom-pom
* Scraps of orange or brown craft foam
* Two wiggle-eyes
* Glue
* Four small feathers

Instructions:

1. Glue pom-pom to the top of the cork. Glue wiggle-eyes to pom-pom and a small triangle of orange craft foam for a beak.

2. Glue the feathers to the sides of the cork. Feathers can also be added to the top of the head.

3. Cut feet from craft foam scraps and glue to the bottom of the cork.

Social Studies:

* State bird
* Birds of a region
* Forest inhabitants

Science:

* Types of owls
* Types of birds
* Bird characteristics

GLUE

Fabric Journal

Materials needed:

* 8 1/2 in. X 11 in. blank paper
* 9 in. X 12 in. fabric scrap
* Scissors
* Glue
* Crayons, markers, or colored
  pencils

Instructions:

1. Fold the blank paper horizontally as shown. Cut the folded edge away, about 1 inch in from either end of the paper.

2. Fold the second sheet in half and cut a slit 1-inch on either end of the fold. This becomes the pages in your journal. (Create more pages if needed.)

3. Fold (but do not crease the page with the slits) in half so that the slits line up.

Social Studies:

* State research
* Textiles and fabrics
* Written response journal

Science:

* Science vocabulary book
* Constellations
* Sound, light, heat journal

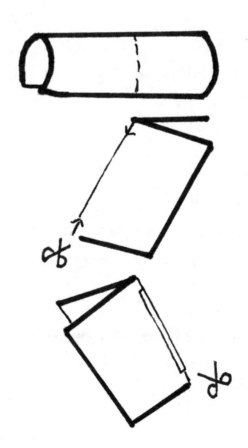

4. Hold the page open with the window in one hand, and insert the folded page with the slits at the top through the window, stopping at the slits. If you want more than one page in your book, insert them all together.

5. Unfold the paper(s) with the slits at the fold to create your finished book.

6. Open the fabric scrap and lay it face down. Lay the open book onto the fabric. Glue the first sheet to the fabric, close the book, and glue the last sheet to the fabric to form a fabric cover.

7. Your fabric journal is now ready to hold illustrations and notes from your unit of study.

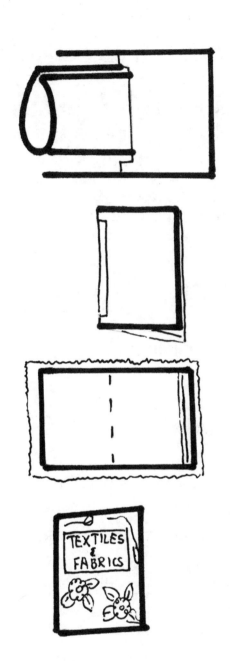

File-Folder Calendar

Materials needed:

* One manila file folder
* Hole-cutter or oval pattern
* Calendar blackline
  (see p. 177)
* Cellophane tape
* Scissors
* Pencils-plain or colored
* Photographs to match unit
* Stapler
* Hole puncher
* String or yarn

Instructions:

1. Using a hole-cutter or oval pattern, cut an oval on the top half of the front page of the manila folder. Be sure that the photo you will use fits behind the oval.

2. Open the folder and tape the photo behind the oval opening that will become the picture frame.

Social Studies:

* Working together
* Dates in history
* Organizing dates

Science:

* Recycling
* Charting growth
* Phases of the moon

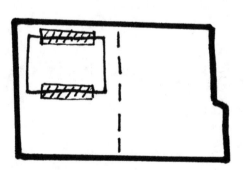

124

3. On the front page of the folder, draw a picture around the photo depicting the topic or unit of study.

4. Staple the calendar blackline to the bottom front half of the manila folder. Add the month, days, dates, and year in pencil.

5. Additional pages can be added for each month of the year. The photo on top can also be changed throughout the year.

6. Punch two holes at the top corners of the file folder and tie string or yarn through each to hang the calendar.

File-Folder Character Walk-Through

Materials needed:

* Manila file folder
* One ice cream stick
* Index card
* Crayons, markers, or colored pencils
* Scissors
* Cellophane tape

Instructions:

1. On the index card, make a side view of a character who will travel through the story. Cut out the character and tape it to the ice cream stick.

2. Fold the file folder in half vertically. Use a ruler to divide the folder into four or five equal sections.

3. Lay the file folder out vertically on the table. Illustrate the top two-thirds of the paper. Write the story along the bottom third.

Social Studies:

* Any historical event
* Sequence historical fiction
* Sequence a timeline

Science:

* Walk-through environment
* Time travel
* Create a science fiction story

4. Refold the folder the original way and cut a line just above the writing, stopping one inch from either outside edge. Cut through only the illustrated side of the paper.

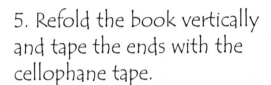

5. Refold the book vertically and tape the ends with the cellophane tape.

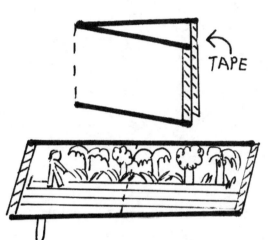

6. Insert the stick puppet through the slit and "walk" through the narrative.

7. Close the file folder and create a cover page to go along with the narrative you have created.

File-Folder Frame

Materials needed:

* One file folder
* Pencil
* Crayons, markers, or colored
  pencils
* Black marker
* Ruler

Social Studies:

* Sequence of events
* Fact organizing
* Study sheet facts

Science:

* Science facts
* Laws of science
* Going on a nature walk

Instructions:

1. Open the file folder and lay
in front of you. Measure a line
four inches up from the
bottom of the folder and fold
along that line.

2. Open the crease and cut the
strip off along the folded edge.

3. Using the ruler, divide the
strip into equal boxes. In each
box, illustrate and write about
a theme or unit of study.

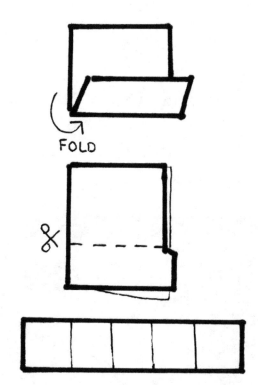

FOLD

4. Close the remaining piece of the folder and draw a box the size of one of the boxes on the file-folder strip.

5. Cut a slit down each vertical side of the box that is a bit longer than the box itself.

6. Cut one more slit along the fold of the folder, parallel to the cut on the left side of the box.

7. Insert the strip from the back of the folder. Go through the right-side slit, out the left-side slit, and finally through the slit on the fold. The strip can now be seen through the open center of the folder.

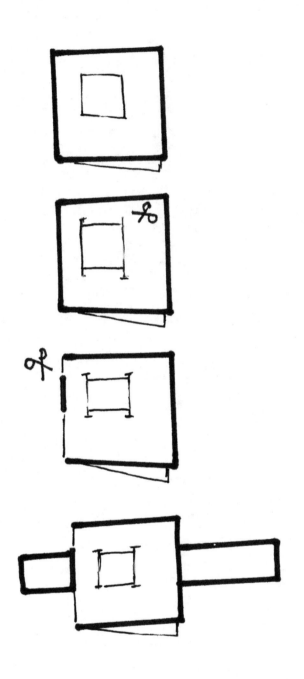

File-Folder Stage

Materials needed:

* One manila file folder
* Scissors
* Crayons, markers, or colored
  pencils
* String, yarn, or twine
* 1 yard survey tape
* Computer-generated
  finger puppets
* Ice cream sticks for each
  finger puppet
* Two pipe cleaners

Instructions:

1. Cut a window approximately
8 1/2 in. X 5 1/2 in. from the
front-center of the file folder.

2. On the inside of the folder,
illustrate the background
scene for your puppet show,
which can be seen through
the window.

3. Hole-punch one hole on
each side at the top of the
illustration. Insert a pipe
cleaner and twist it into a loop.

Social Studies:

* Civil War units
* Debate
* Pioneers

Science:

* Scientist/discovery
* Science Fair topics
* Environments/animals

CUT OUT

4. Put the survey tape around your neck and place the file folder stage in front of you. Slip the ends of the survey tape through each loop and tie the ends around each pipe cleaner.

5. Tie a piece of string from each hole at the bottom of the frame and again to the loops at the top. The puppet stage is now ready to be used.

6. Use the computer to find clip art characters that can be used in your puppet show. Cut closely around each figure and tape them to a ice cream stick.

7. Your puppets and stage are now ready to be used to perform your unit.

Journal-in-a-Tube

Materials needed:

* Long cardboard tube from
  paper towels or gift wrap
* Heavy brown paper
* Crayons, markers, or colored
  pencils
* Glue
* Scissors
* Paper stapled together as a
  journal
* Scraps of twine, beads,
  feathers, foam, and gift wrap
* Hole puncher

Instructions:

1. Decorate the heavy brown
paper and glue or tape to the
outside of the tube. Tie scraps
of twine to either end and add
beads and feathers to the ends
of the tube.

2. Using the paper stapled
together as a journal, design a
cover to go along with the
topic or unit of study.

Social Studies:

* Geography journal
* Early Americans journal
* Cultural mapping journal

Science:

* Field trip journal
* Experiment journal
* Charts and graphs journal

3. Hole punch the edge of the journal and attach twine or string long enough to stick out of the end of the tube. Feathers or beads can also be added to decorate the string.

4. Carefully roll the journal tight enough to fit inside of the tube. Be sure to allow the string to hang out of the end of the tube so the journal can be pulled out easily.

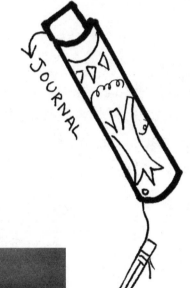

* Optional: Add a small pencil or pen to the string—your journal is ready to travel with you.

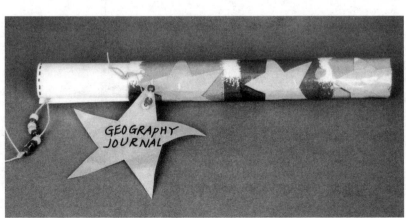

Mini-Envelope Bag

Materials needed:

* One business-size envelope
* One pipe cleaner
* Adding machine paper
* Crayons, markers, or colored pencils
* Cellophane tape
* Hole puncher
* Scissors

Instructions:

1. Seal the envelope and cut it in half from top to bottom. Fold the sides back and forth and crease the bottom back and forth.

2. Put your hand in the envelope and flatten the bottom. Fold two points on the bottom corners of the bag, and tape them flat to the bottom of the bag.

3. Pinch the sides of the bag in to create folded sides of the bag. Make two 1/2 in. slits across the bottom of the bag about one inch from the bottom front side.

Social Studies:

* U.S. landforms
* What comes next?
* Years in history

Science:

* Vocabulary
* Hypothesis/conclusion
* True/false

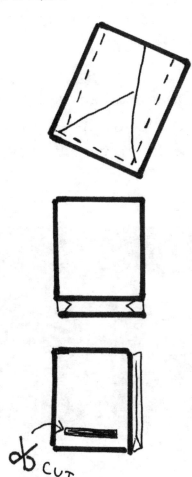

CUT

4. On adding-machine tape, write questions and answers or facts.

5. Roll the adding machine tape, insert in the bag, and bring it through the slit in the front. Cut the ends of the paper into a point so it is easier to pull through the bag.

6. Punch four holes at the top of the bag and insert pipe cleaners to make handles.

No-Glue Paper Plate Book

Materials needed:

* Two paper plates
  (cheap ones)
* Crayons, markers, or colored
  pencils
* Scissors

Social Studies:

* Comparing two regions
* Continents
* States

Science:

* Pond life/ocean life
* Deserts/mountains
* Arctic/Antarctica

Instructions:

1. Fold the first paper plate in half and cut a narrow window out of the folded edge. Start the window after the ruffled edge and end before the other ruffled edge.

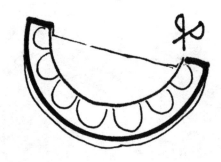

2. Fold the second paper plate in half and open. On the fold, cut one slit from the edge of the plate to the end of the ruffle (about one inch long). Make a second slit directly opposite the first one.

3. Fold (but do not crease) the paper plate with the slits in half so that the two slits meet. With the plate folded in half, push the plate through the slit. Open the plate, moving one slit to the top of the window and one slit to the bottom of the window.

4. Close the booklet so all the plates are folded in half. Label the front cover to match theme of unit. On each page of the book, comparisons can be made—one view on the top half and another on the bottom half of each page.

* The number of pages in this book can be increased by making more paper plates with the slits on the ends and inserting them through the window at the same time.

Pants' Pocket Book

Materials needed:

* Fabric paint in assorted colors
* One piece of tagboard the same size as pocket
* Hole puncher
* Scissors
* Two keychain loops or chicken rings
* Back pocket from an old pair of denim jeans (two pieces)
* 5-10 pieces of paper cut the same size as the pocket
* Crayons, markers, or colored pencils
* Glue

Instructions:

1. Glue extra piece of denim to tagboard to create the back pocket.

Social Studies:

* All about the West
* Western settlements
* Picture dictionary

Science:

* United States crops
* Light, heat, sound energy
* Materials used for textiles

2. Stack front cover, inside pages, and back cover and mark with a pen for the placement of rings. Punch holes through the pages and back cover, then push rings through the pocket, inside pages, and back cover. Secure closed.

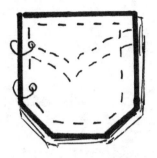

3. Front cover can now be decorated with fabric paint to show the main idea of the unit or theme.

4. Use the pocket in the front to store crayons, markers, and pencils that will be used to write in the journal.

Slide Samples

Materials needed:

* 3 in. X 5 in. white, unlined
  index card
* Clear, wide packaging tape
* Empty 35mm container
* Scissors
* Pencil or pen
* Soil

Instructions:

1. Have students each take
home a 35mm film container
and collect some soil to be
brought back to school.

2. Fold the 3 in. X 5 in. index
card in half horizontally
(hamburger fold).

3. Cut a "V" shape out of the
folded edge as shown. When
the index card is opened it
should have a diamond shape.

Social Studies:

* Areas of soil types
* Deserts
* Farming in America

Science:

* Layers of soil
* Life in soil
* Kinds of soil

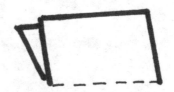

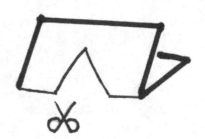

4. Place a piece of clear, wide packaging tape over the diamond-shaped opening.

5. Sprinkle some soil over the sticky side of the tape peeping through the diamond-shaped opening. Shake off the excess soil, leaving only what remains on the tape.

6. Cover the soil side of the slide with another piece of packaging tape.

7. Label the slide with information about where the soil was found. Use a microscope or magnifying glass to get a closer look at the soil sample.

Two-Sided Accordion Pictures

Materials needed:

* Manila file folder
* Two pictures of a similar size and theme
* Glue
* Scissors
* Ruler
* Pencil

Instructions:

1. Flip picture over to the back side. Using the ruler measure, draw vertical strips across the back of the picture, one-inch apart.

2. At the bottom of each strip, label in order: 1A, 1B, 1C, etc. Cut the strips apart.

3. Using the other picture, repeat steps 1 and 2, except label the strips 2A, 2B, 2C, etc.

Social Studies:

* Map/scenic view
* Photo/portrait
* Cityscape/countryscape

Science:

* Day/night scene
* Animal: young/adult
* Above/underground

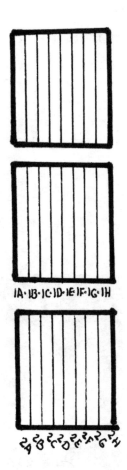

1A·1B·1C·1D·1E·1F·1G·1H

4. Cut the edge of the file folder away to create a large rectangle when open. Draw lines down the file folder 1-inch apart. Label the strips 1A, 2A, 1B, 2B, etc. Match the picture strips to the strips on the file folder and glue.

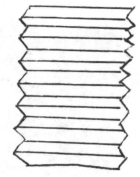

5. Accordion-fold the file folder/picture. You will see a different view from the right side and left side of the picture.

Project Blacklines

Using the Blacklines

We began The Bag Ladies ten years ago because of teacher demand for hands-on projects that would apply standards within all content areas of the curriculum. These teachers did not want to create the ideas, so we did it for them. We realized that they wanted not only the activity, with step-by-step directions, but also ways to apply the standards, as well as blacklines to run off for each student. This section includes blacklines for many of the activities with suggestions for using them.

Years ago, if we gave students a blackline to complete, we got back projects that all looked alike. Students would do the work, but the results were less than creative. Today, this is not the norm. Students are willing to take risks with the projects, be creative, and even add their own ideas. We like the blacklines because they make it easier for the teacher to present the project and for students to have a place to begin.

Helpful Hints

* Change the size of the blacklines. Students like projects that are larger than the everyday paper they use, so mix up the sizes of the projects by enlarging some of them and reducing others.

* Use colored copy paper to run off the blacklines. White paper works very well for some of the projects, but the colored copy paper adds more variety and interest. Students can use Gel FX Markers on the colored paper to make the project illustrations stand out. Colored copy paper is also cheaper than the colored construction paper. You can even run different colors of the same blackline so students can choose.

* Run more than one copy for students. Students will make more than one project. Some students will save the paper to work on extra credit, and others will take it home to continue the same objectives. Also, the projects should be risk-free. Encourage students to use pencil first, then outline and color in. But, if students should make a mistake or lose their project pages, it is good to have extras nearby.

* Use the blacklines for making the actual models that you will share with the students.

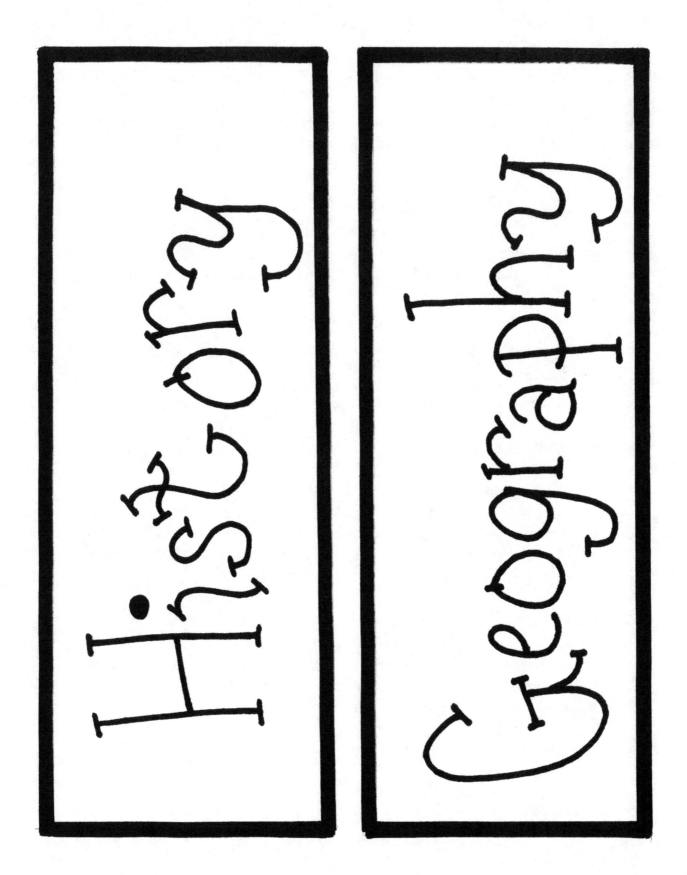

Folder Holder Social Studies Labels-2

Social Studies
Projects

Social Studies
Notes

Lab Work

Science Notes

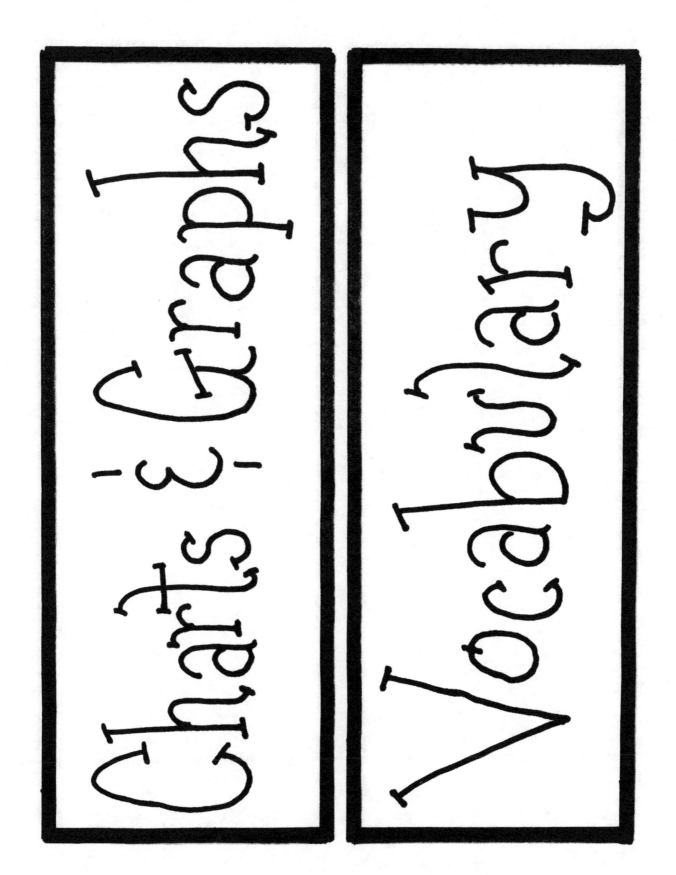

Charts & Graphs

Vocabulary

Folder-Holder Blank Labels

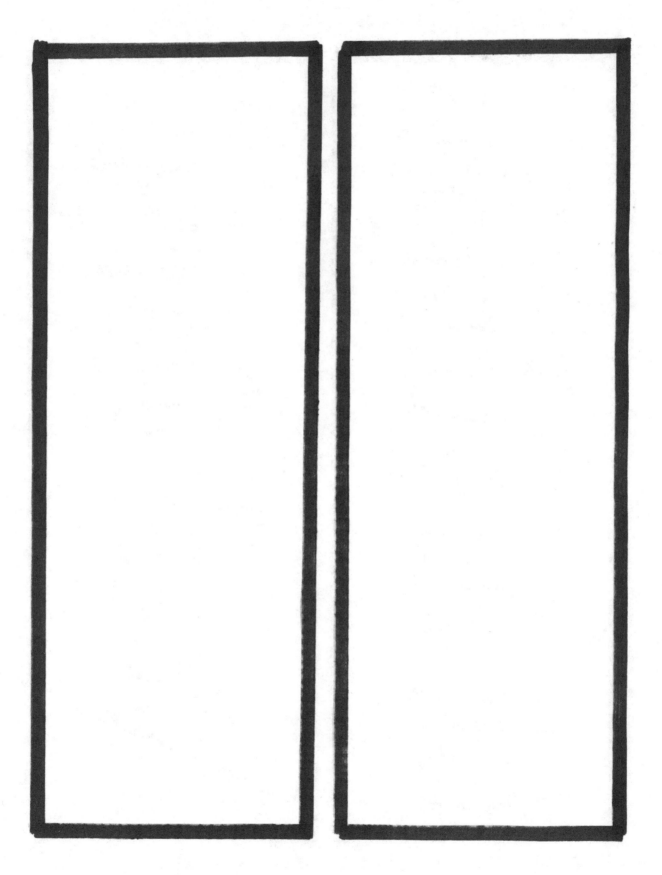

Brown-Bag Stage

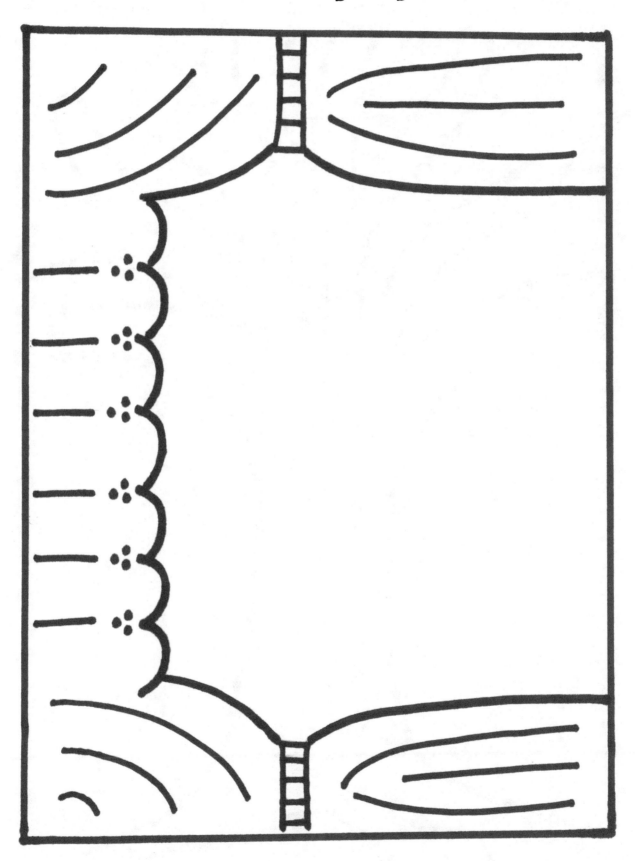

Double-Pocket Tree

Double-Pocket Ship

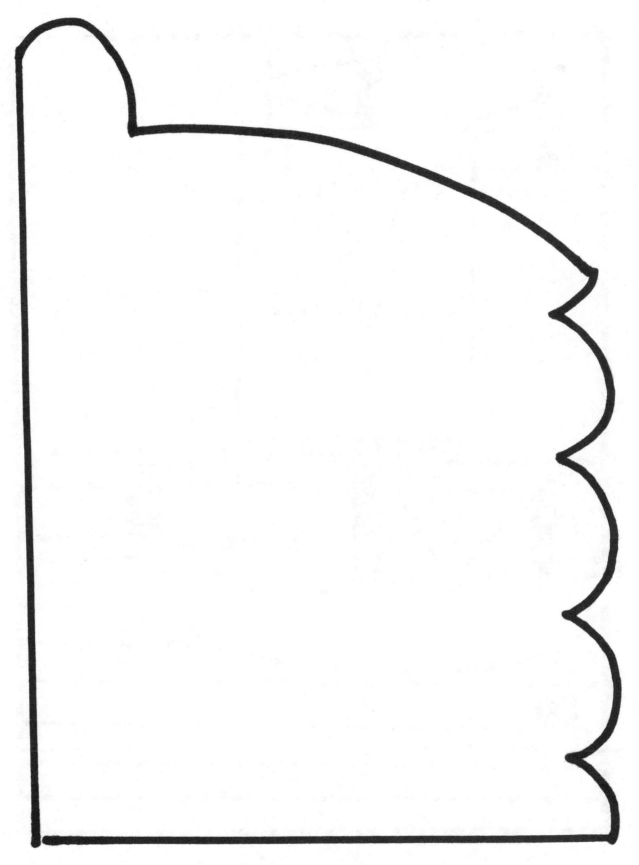

Double-Pocket Ship Book Cover

My Story
about

_____

NAME

DATE

Step-n-Pocket Bag: Side One Labels

What does my Earth have?

My Earth has forests.

My Earth has deserts.

My Earth has rain forests.

My Earth has oceans.

My Earth has Arctic regions.

My Earth has mountains.

My Earth has forests, deserts, rain forests, oceans, Arctic regions, mountains, and me!

Step-n-Pocket Bag: Side One Labels

Step-n-Pocket Bag: Side One Labels

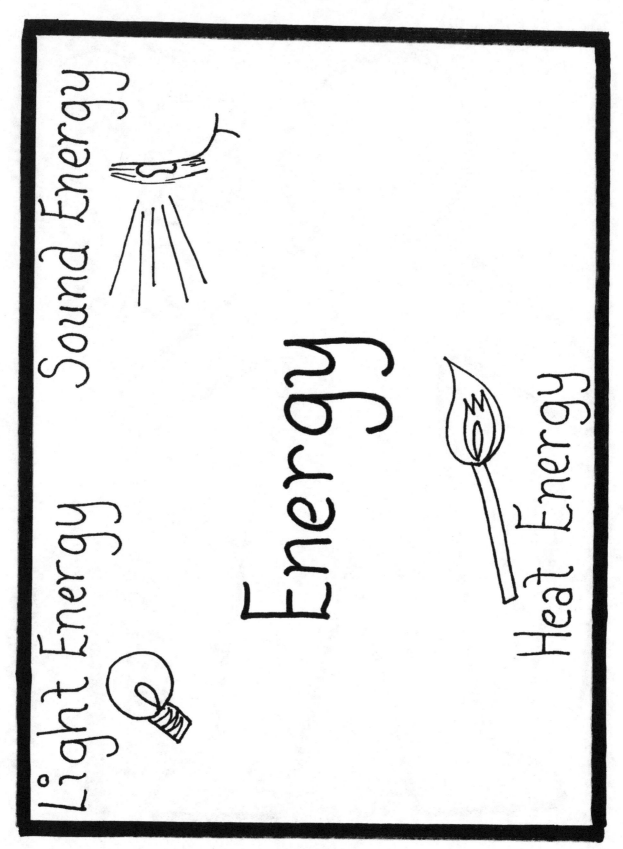

Thanksgiving Bag Horn-of-Plenty

I am thankful for...

Thanksgiving Bag Turkey

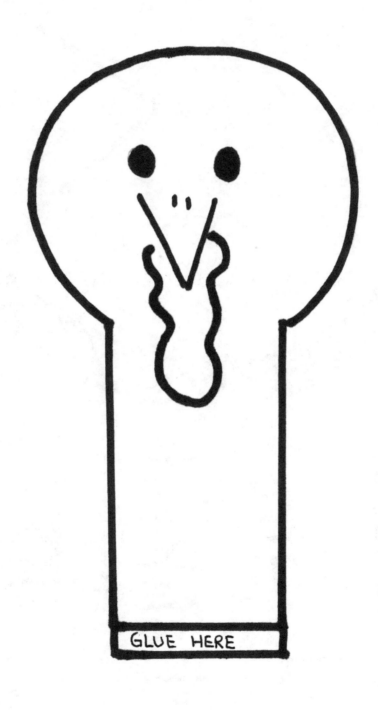

GLUE HERE

Timeline Bag-1

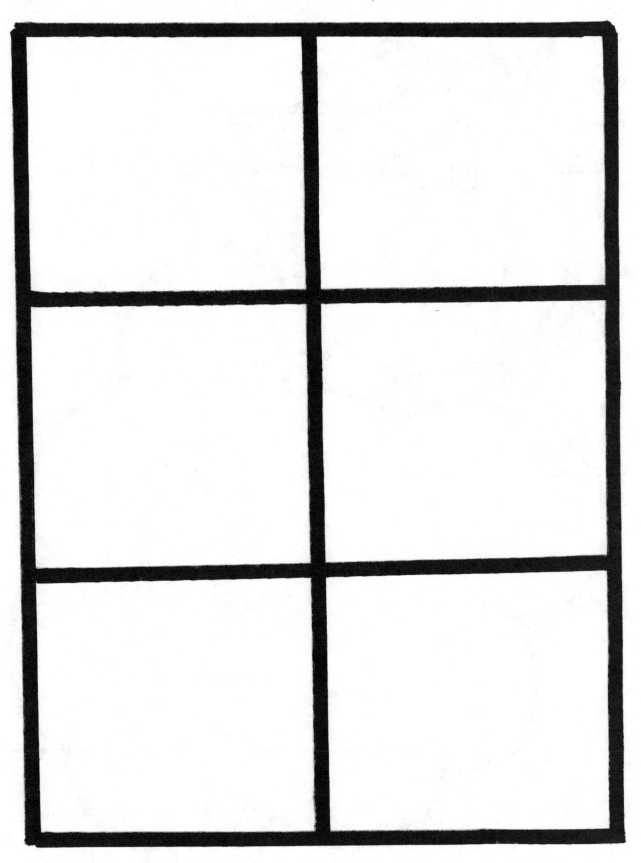

Timeline Bag-2

Band-Aids

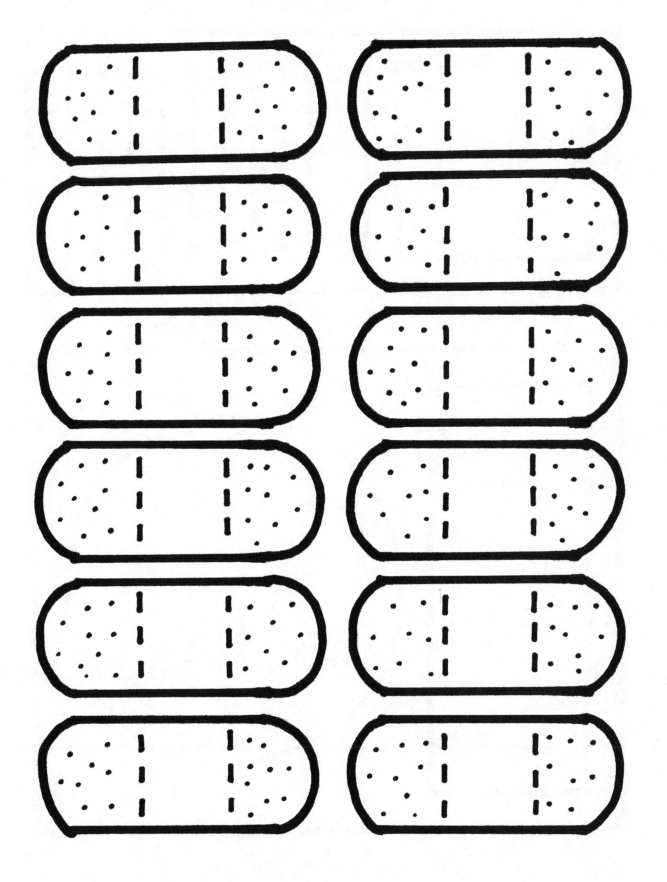

Cereal Box–1

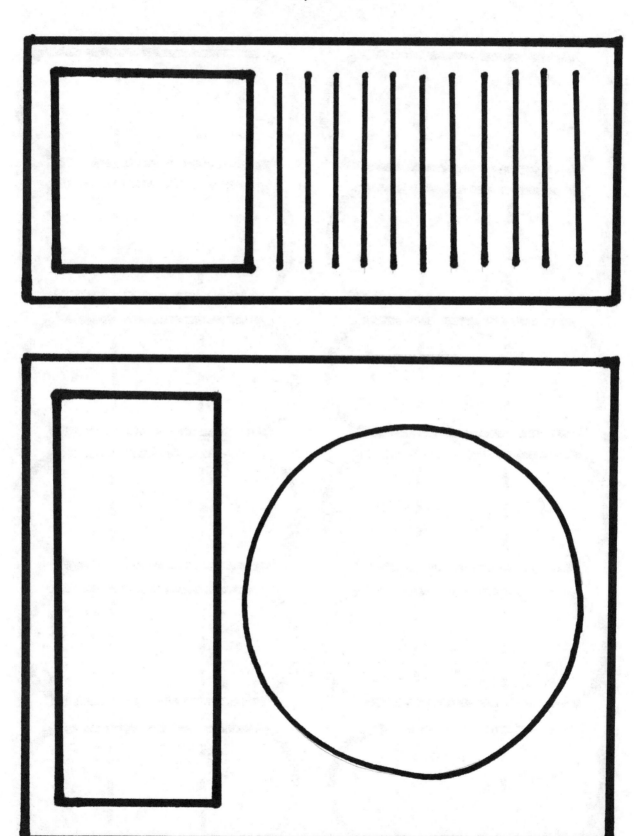

Cereal Box-2

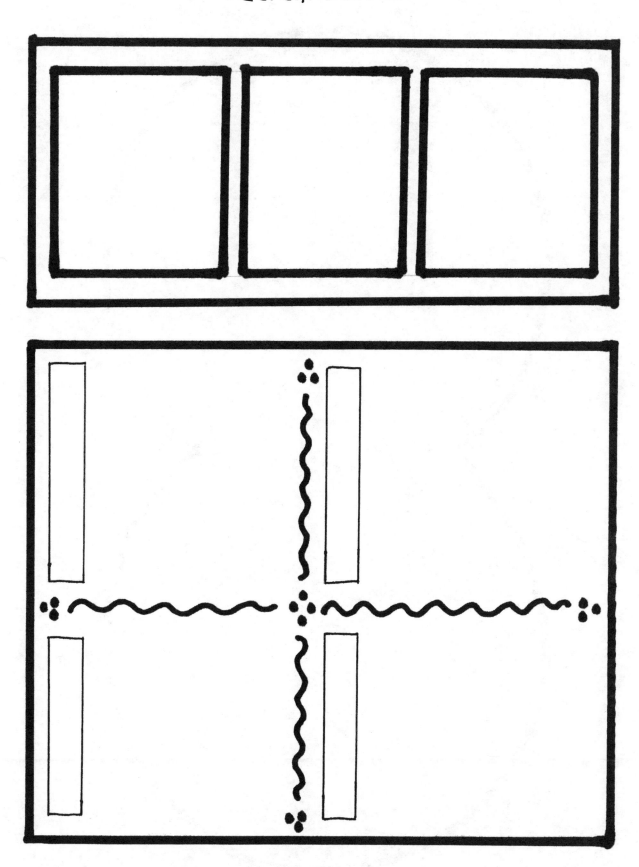

CD Accordion Book

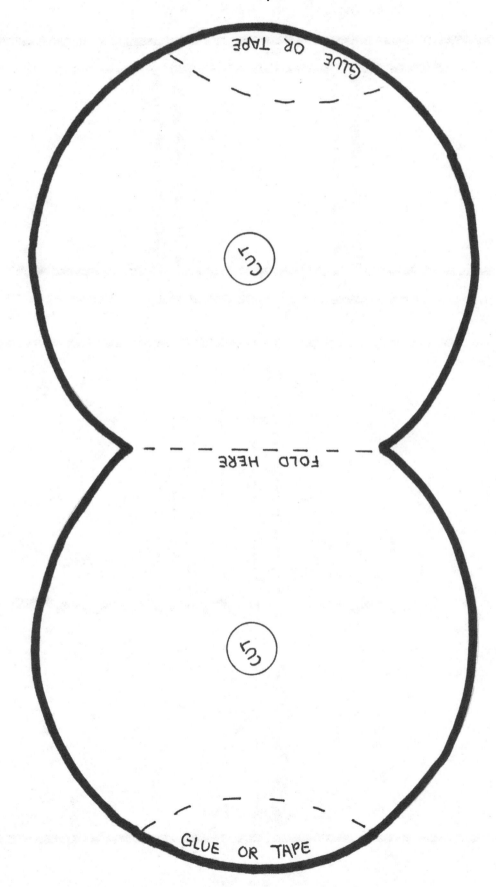

Food Box Suitcase-1

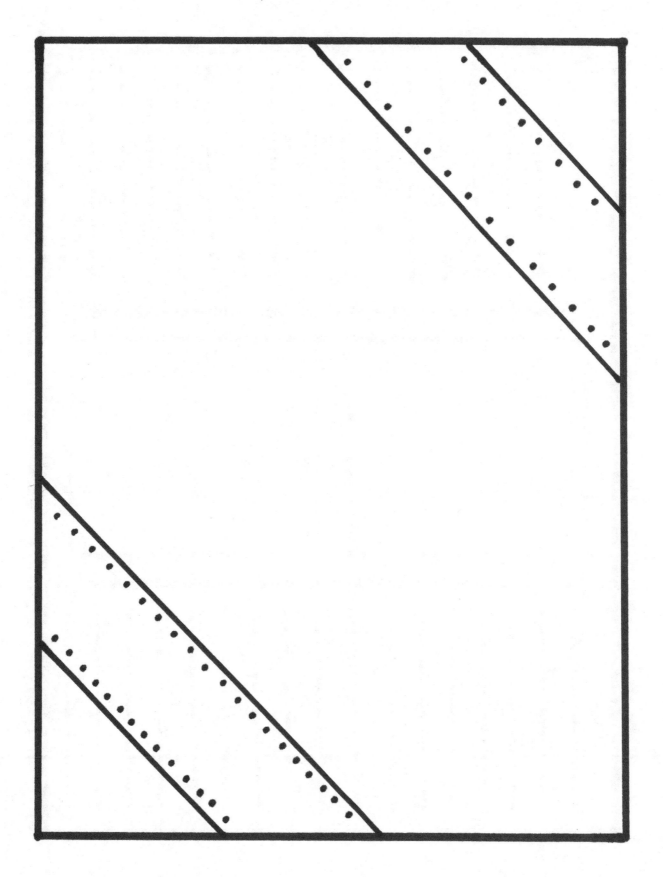

Food Box Suitcase-2

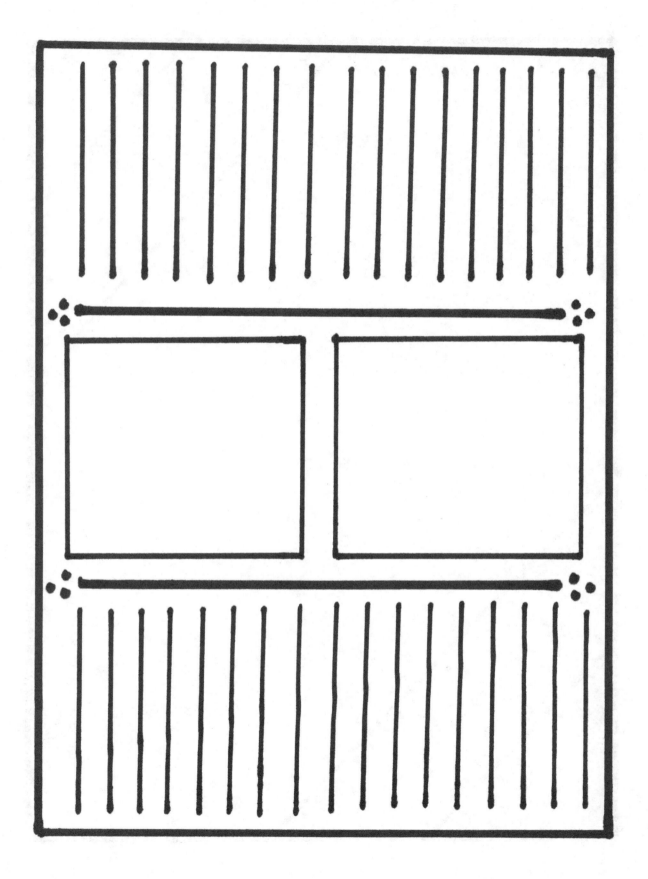

Pizza Box Game Board-1

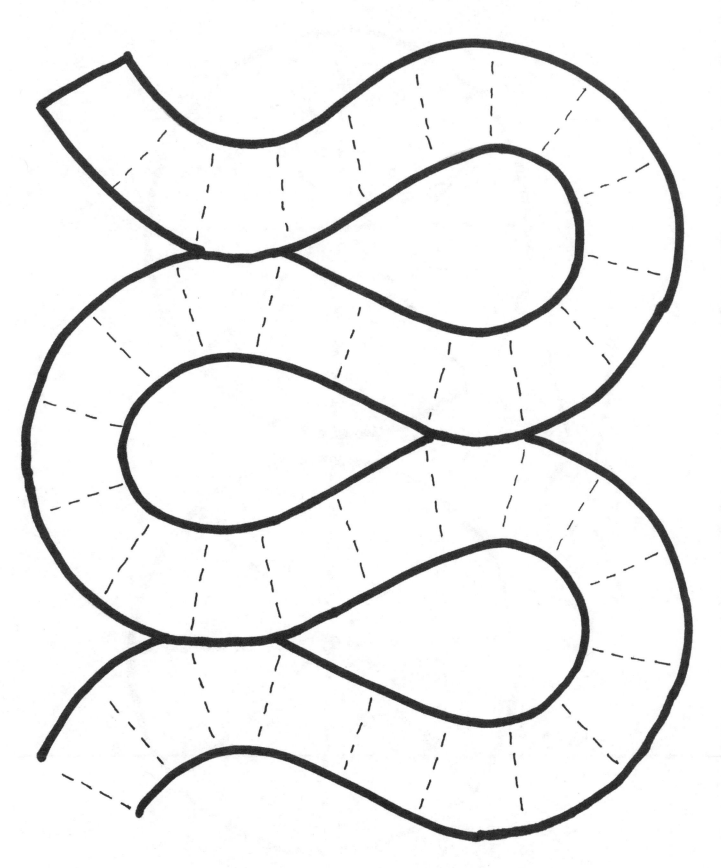

Pizza Box Game Board-2

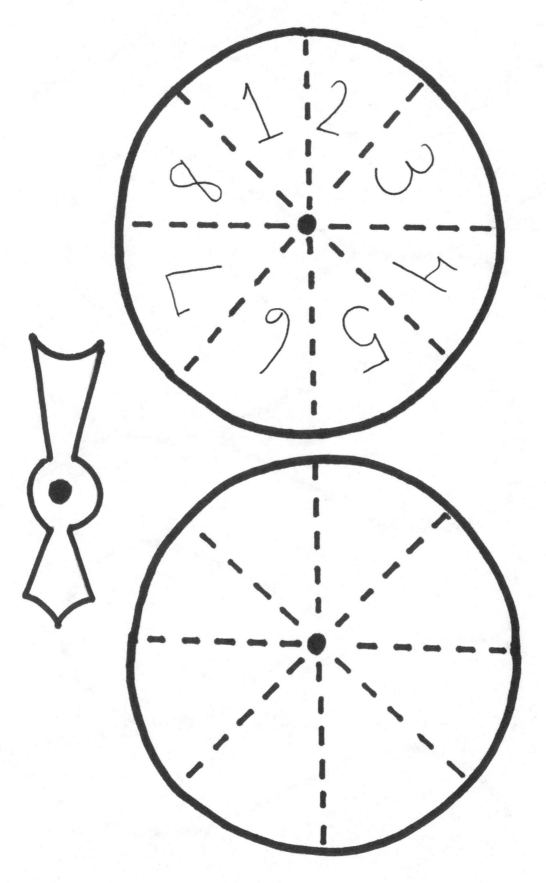

Take-Out Container Box-1

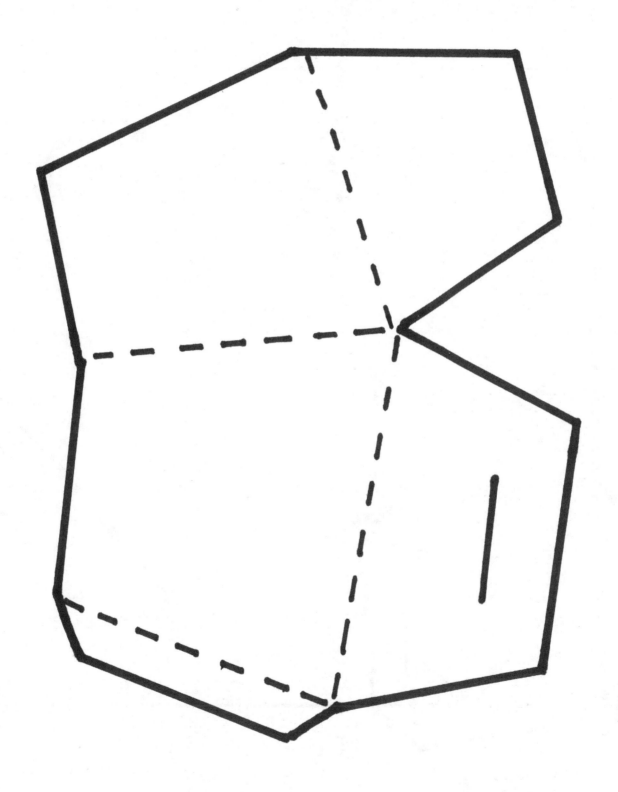

Take-Out Container Box-2

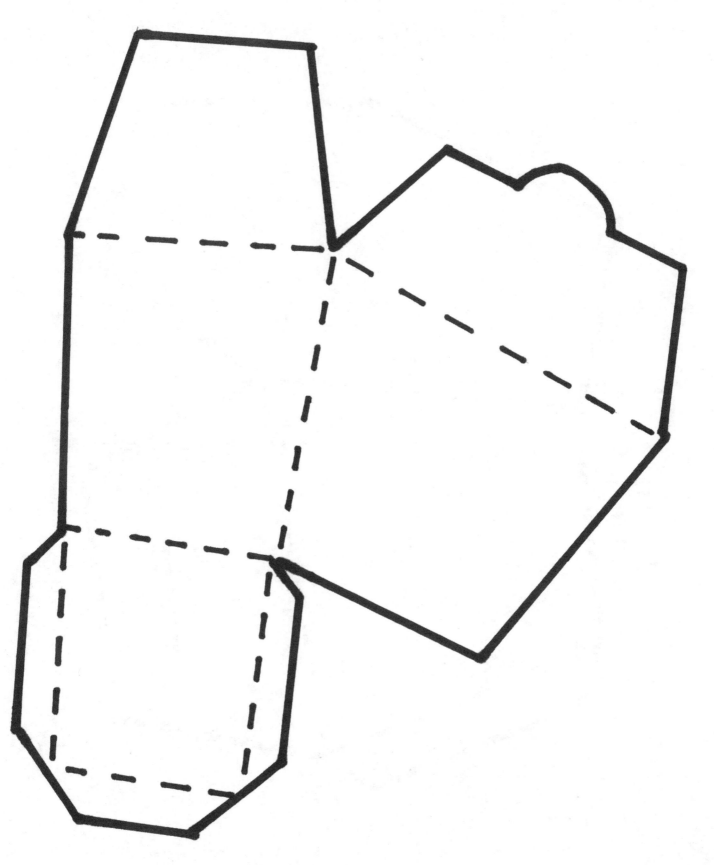

Camera-Shaped Book-1

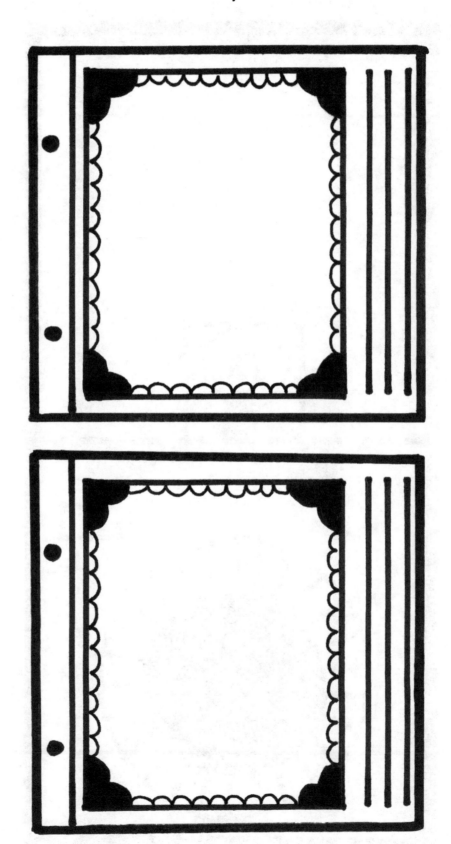

Camera-Shaped Book-2

File-Folder Calendar

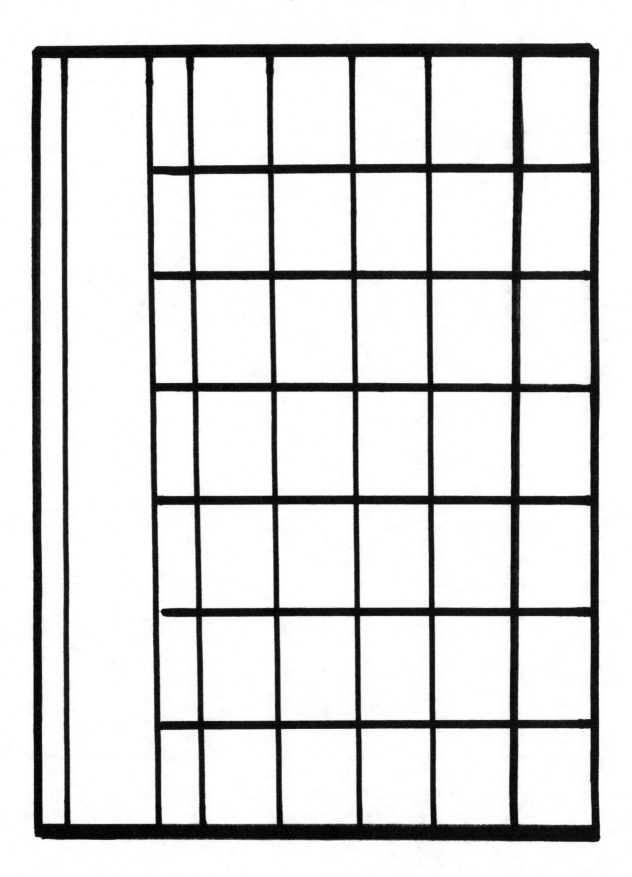

Bag Lady Contact Information

Quantity	Title	Price	Tax	Total
_____	A Mathsquerade for the Millennium and Beyond	17.00	1.02	_____
_____	A Walk Across Florida	17.00	1.02	_____
_____	Ants, Bats, and Other Creatures	17.00	1.02	_____
_____	Anytime is Summertime	17.00	1.02	_____
_____	Book Talks	17.00	1.02	_____
_____	Castles, Characters, and Kaleidoscopes	17.00	1.02	_____
_____	Exciting Egg Experiences	17.00	1.02	_____
_____	Hats Off to the USA	17.00	1.02	_____
_____	How Does Your Garden Grow?	17.00	1.02	_____
_____	Kids, Colors, and Quilts	17.00	1.02	_____
_____	Lights, Cameras, Shadows, Action	17.00	1.02	_____
_____	No Nonsense Non-Fiction	17.00	1.02	_____
_____	Picking Up After the Picnic	17.00	1.02	_____
_____	Poetry Pouch	17.00	1.02	_____
_____	Positively Perfect Projects	17.00	1.02	_____
_____	Readin' Ritin' and Rithmetic	17.00	1.02	_____
_____	Secret Stories Classroom Phonics Kit	84.95	5.09	_____
_____	Turn Your Classroom into an Egyptian Museum	17.00	1.02	_____
_____	Under the Ground, On the Ground, Above the Ground	17.00	1.02	_____
_____	Up In the Air	17.00	1.02	_____
_____	Writing Thoughts	17.00	1.02	_____
_____	Miss Jenny's Science CD	17.00	1.02	_____
_____	Miss Jenny's Math CD	17.00	1.02	_____
_____	Miss Jenny's Math Kit (including CD)	24.95	1.50	_____
_____	Miss Jenny's Think Time CD	10.00	.60	_____

Subtotal _____

Add 10% shipping/handling _____

Total _____

Ship to: _____

Address: _____

_____ Phone: _____

City/State/Zip: _____ Email: _____

The Bag Ladies, PMB 162, 2336 S. East Ocean Blvd. Stuart, FL 34996-3310
Phone: 772-781-2518 or 772-463-1420
Web site: bagladiesonline.com / Email: bladies123@aol.com